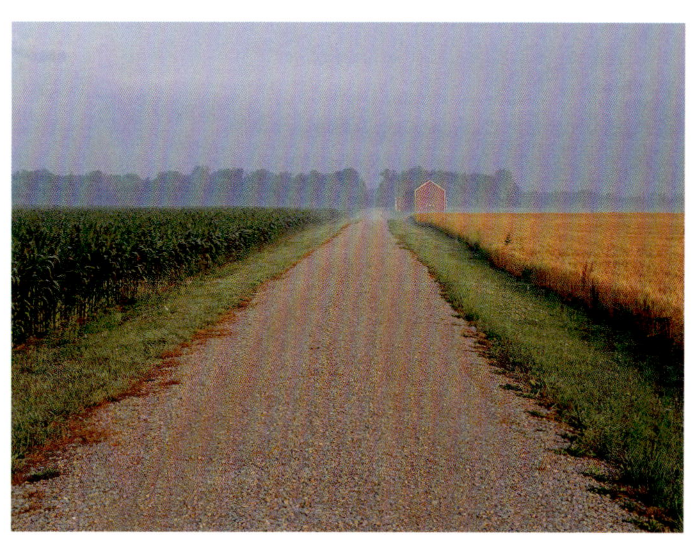

OHIO

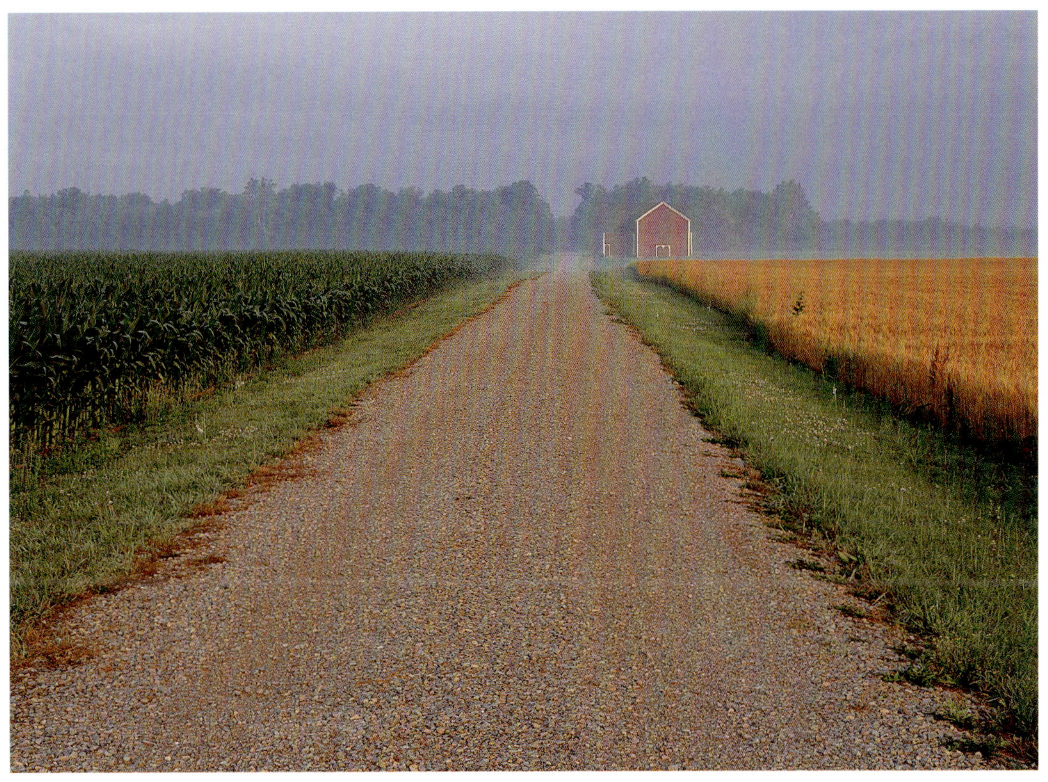

WHITECAP BOOKS

Second printing, 2005

Text by Tanya Lloyd
Edited by Elaine Jones
Photo editing by Tanya Lloyd
Proofread by Lisa Collins
Cover and interior design by Maxine Lea

Printed and bound in Canada

National Library of Canada Cataloguing in Publication Data

Lloyd, Tanya, 1973–
Ohio

(America series)
ISBN 1-55285-176-1

1. Ohio—Pictorial works. I. Title. II. Series: Lloyd, Tanya, 1973- America series.
F492.L56 2001 977.1'044'0222 C2001-910268-2

The publisher acknowledges the financial support of the Government of Canada through the Book Publishing Industry Development Program for our publishing activities.

For more information on the America Series and other Whitecap Books titles, please visit our web site at www.whitecap.ca.

Some states offer replicas of fur-trading forts from the new frontier or sites from the Revolutionary War. But Ohio's history stretches far beyond the time when European explorers picked a route across the continent. Even before the Roman Empire, this region, rich in fruit and fur, was home to the Adena people. They left behind hints of their culture in the buried tools and sculpted mounds they created.

Later, it was the Miami and the Shawnee who harvested Ohio's forests and fished its rivers. They knew what European settlers were soon to discover — this was a paradise of rich soil and abundant water. In fact, half of Ohio is prime farmland, and the new settlers from England, Germany and around the world were quick to begin the harvest. In the nineteenth century, towns sprang up across the state, steel mills followed grist mills, and goods swept their way to market on newly built railways and canals. Soon, the one-time land of the Adena was the State of Ohio, rich in talent and resources.

Today, Ohio's 40,953 square miles are home to more than 11 million residents. The state has grown into a patchwork of rich farmland and cultural centers, bustling port towns and gentle, winding rivers. Some regions, such as the Little Miami River Valley with its lush parkland and shaded trails, remain much as they were in the early nineteenth century. Others have grown to meet the challenges of the present. Sightseers fill the streets of Cincinnati, lawmakers walk the halls of the State Capitol in Columbus, and architects reinvent the skyline of Cleveland. For visitors and residents, Ohio offers an array of sights and attractions, some commemorating a rich history and some celebrating a promising future.

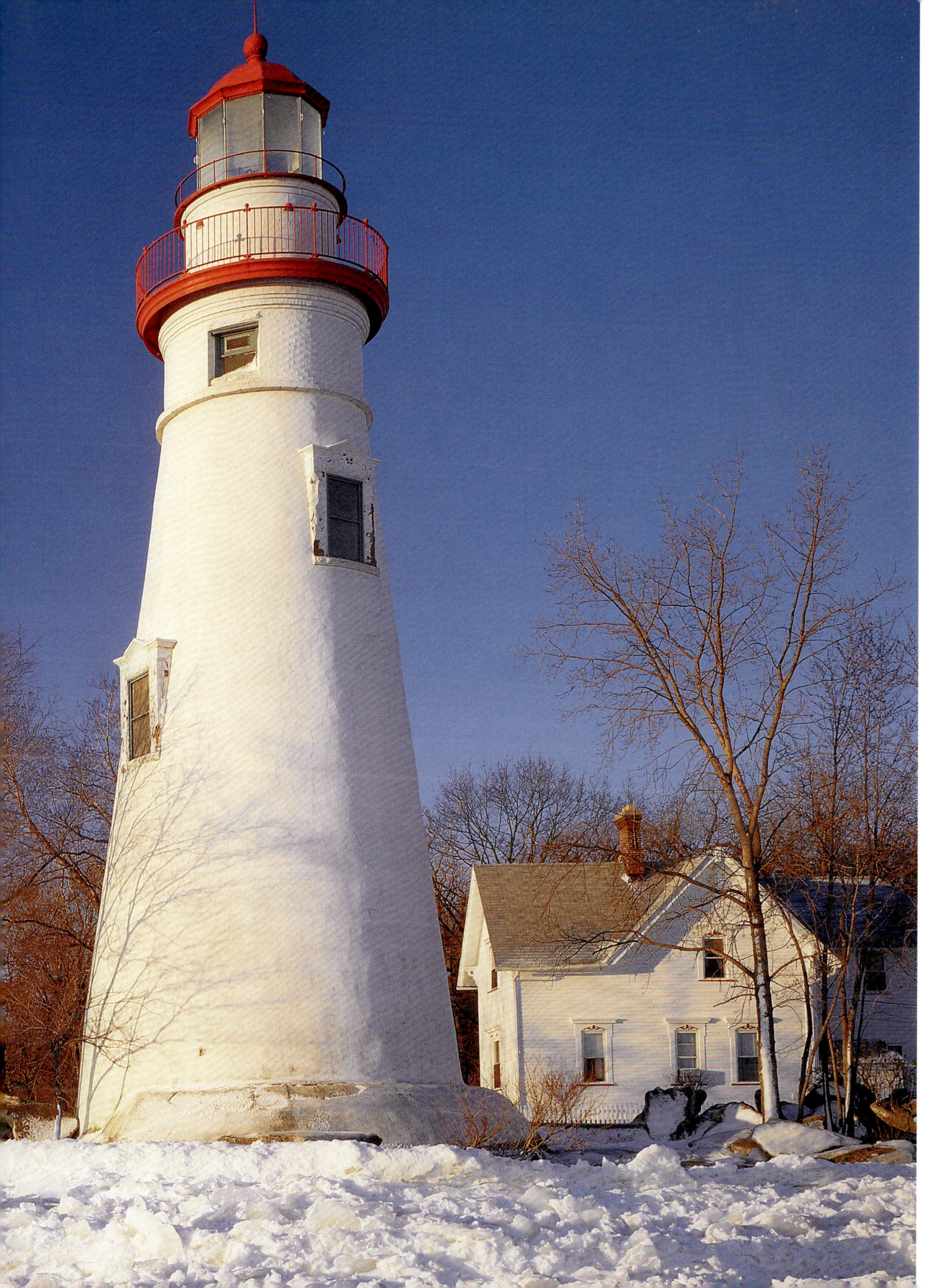

Benajah Wolcott was the first person to tend the Marblehead Lighthouse on the shores of Lake Erie in 1822. The original beacon consisted of thirteen whale-oil lamps. When Wolcott died in 1832, his wife, Rachel, took over the position, one of two women keepers in the history of the lighthouse.

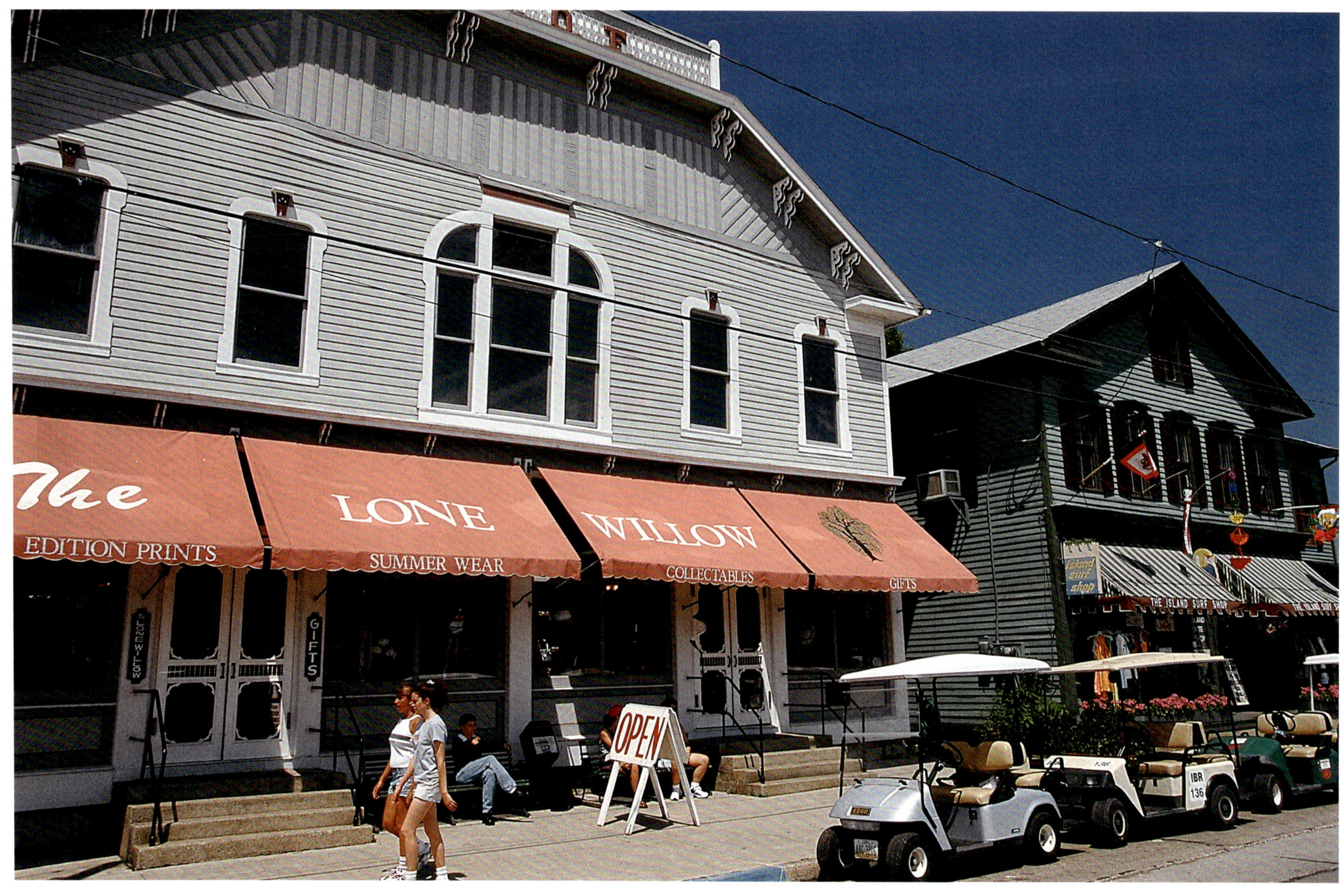

Just off the shores of South Bass Island, American soldiers captured a British fleet in one of the pivotal battles of the War of 1812. The island's small community, Put-in-Bay, earned its name for the refuge it offered from Lake Erie storms — sailing vessels could put in for shelter.

Tempting summer visitors inside with its quaint decor and colorful displays, the Wileswood Country Store in Huron offers popcorn and old-fashioned candy.

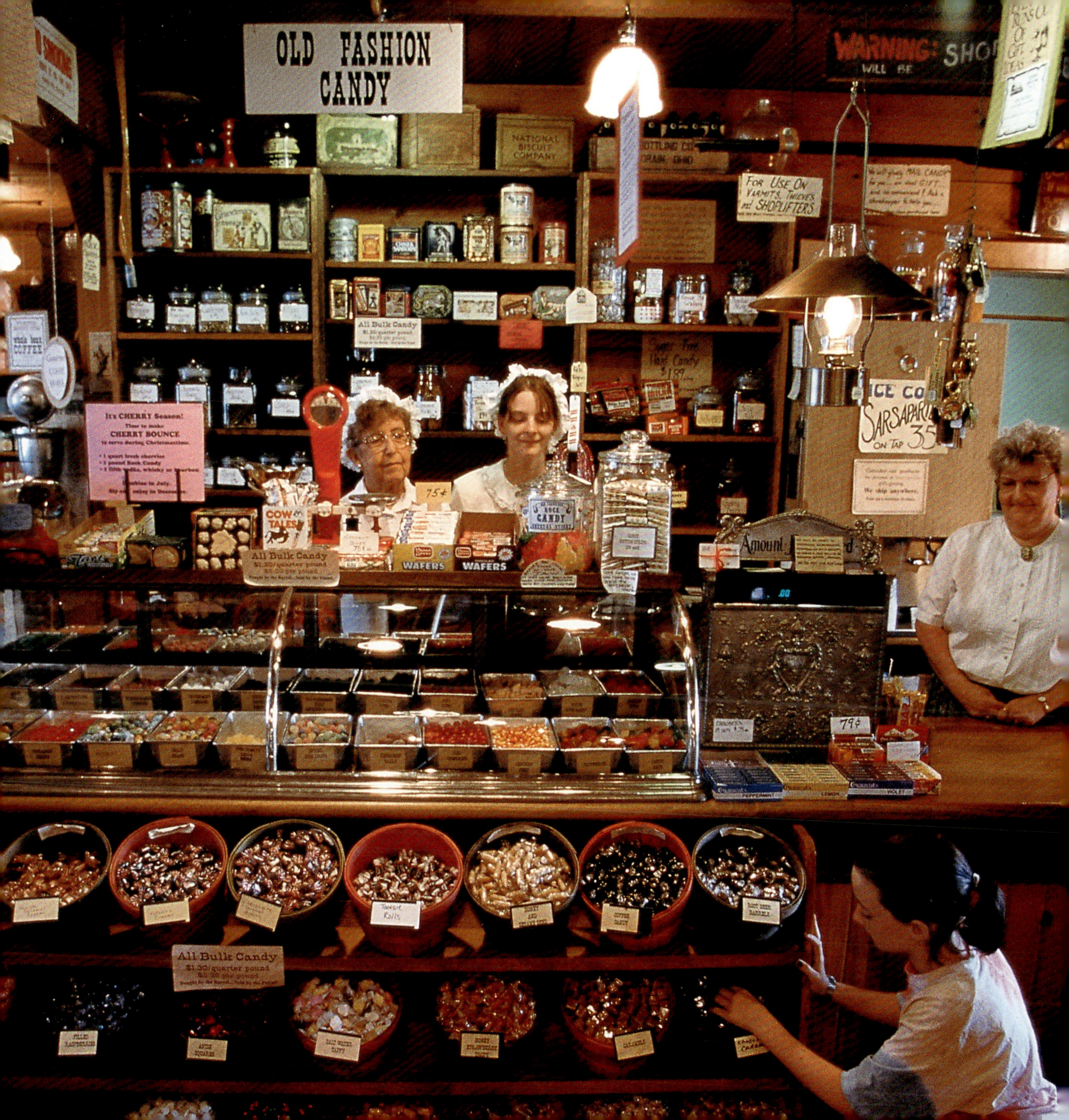

OLD FASHION CANDY
WARNING:
NATIONAL BISCUIT COMPANY
FOR USE ON VARMITS, THIEVES and SHOPLIFTERS
All Bulk Candy
It's CHERRY Season!
CHERRY BOUNCE
COW TALES
75¢
WAFERS
WAFERS
ROCK CANDY
ON TAP 35
79¢
Tootsie Rolls
All Bulk Candy

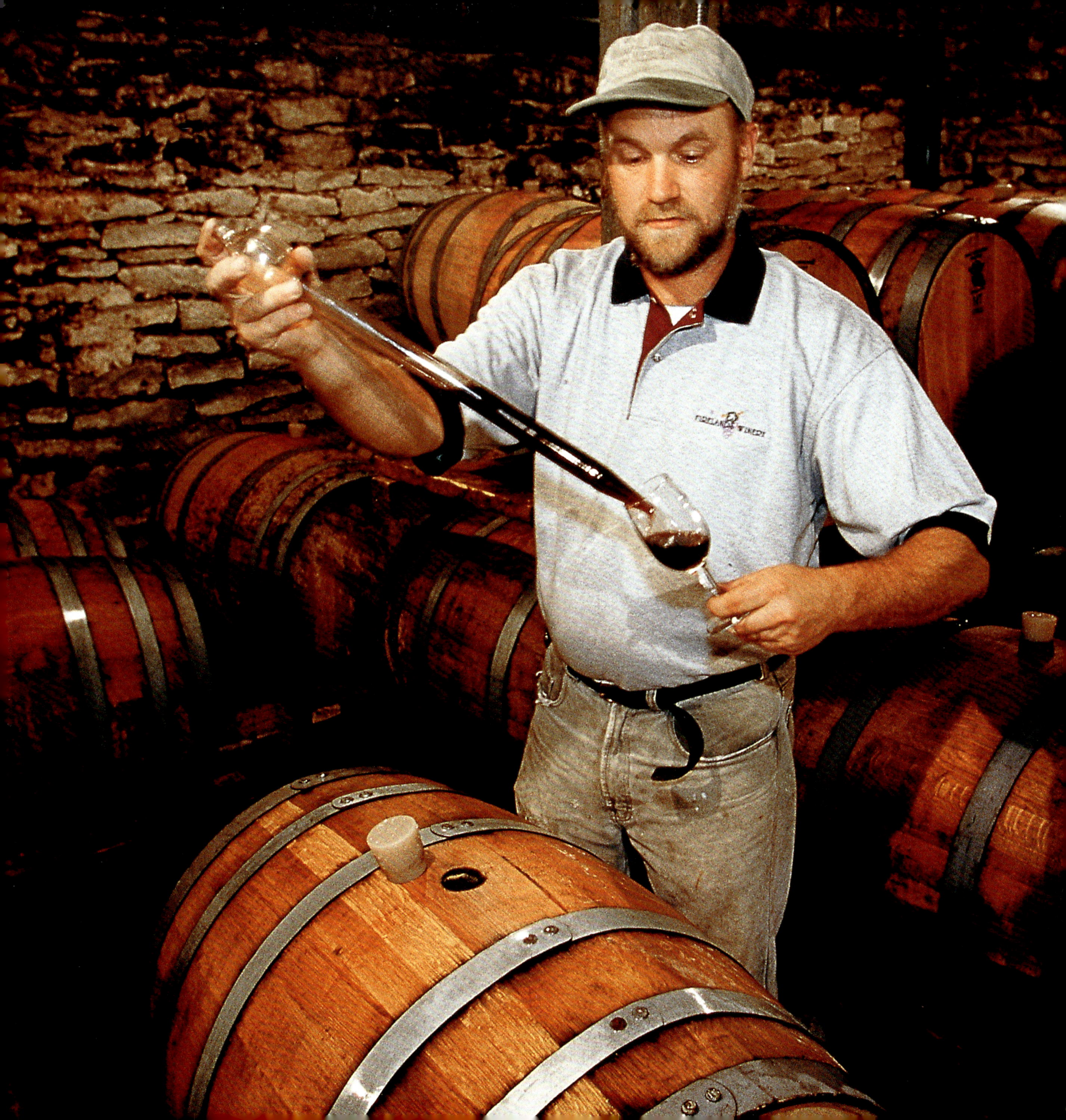

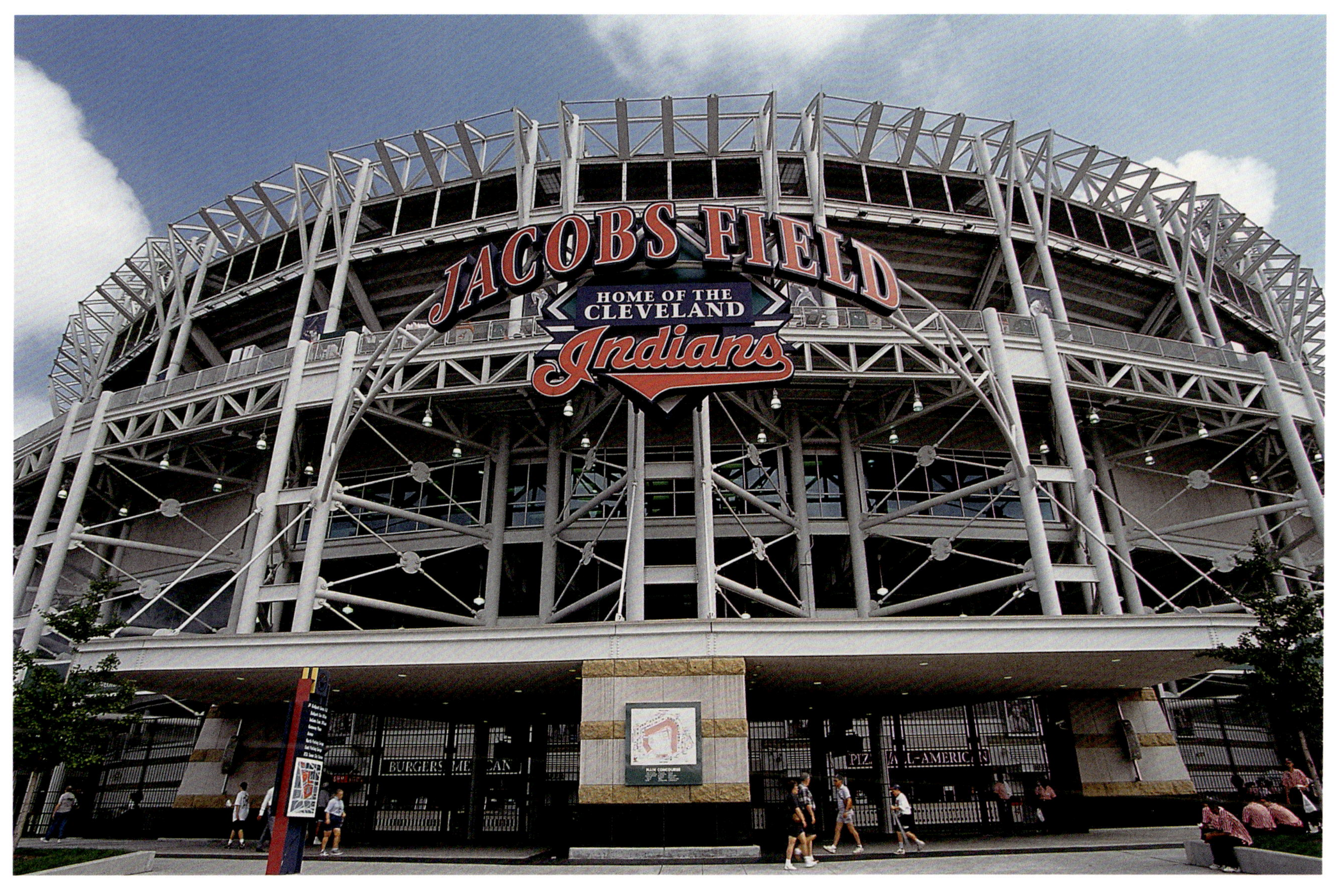

Since Jacobs Field opened in 1994, the Cleveland Indians have enjoyed an enviable record, selling out almost 300 consecutive games and boosting the local economy by an estimated $500 million.

After the Revolutionary War, Connecticut residents who had lost their homes to the British settled on the shores of Lake Erie. The temperate climate, moderated by the lake waters, allowed settler Edward Mantey to begin producing unique vintages at Firelands Winery in 1880.

Cleveland is a collection of distinct neighborhoods. From the cafés of Little Italy and the galleries of Tremont to the antique stores of Shaker Square and the gardens of Glenville, each area has its own appeal.

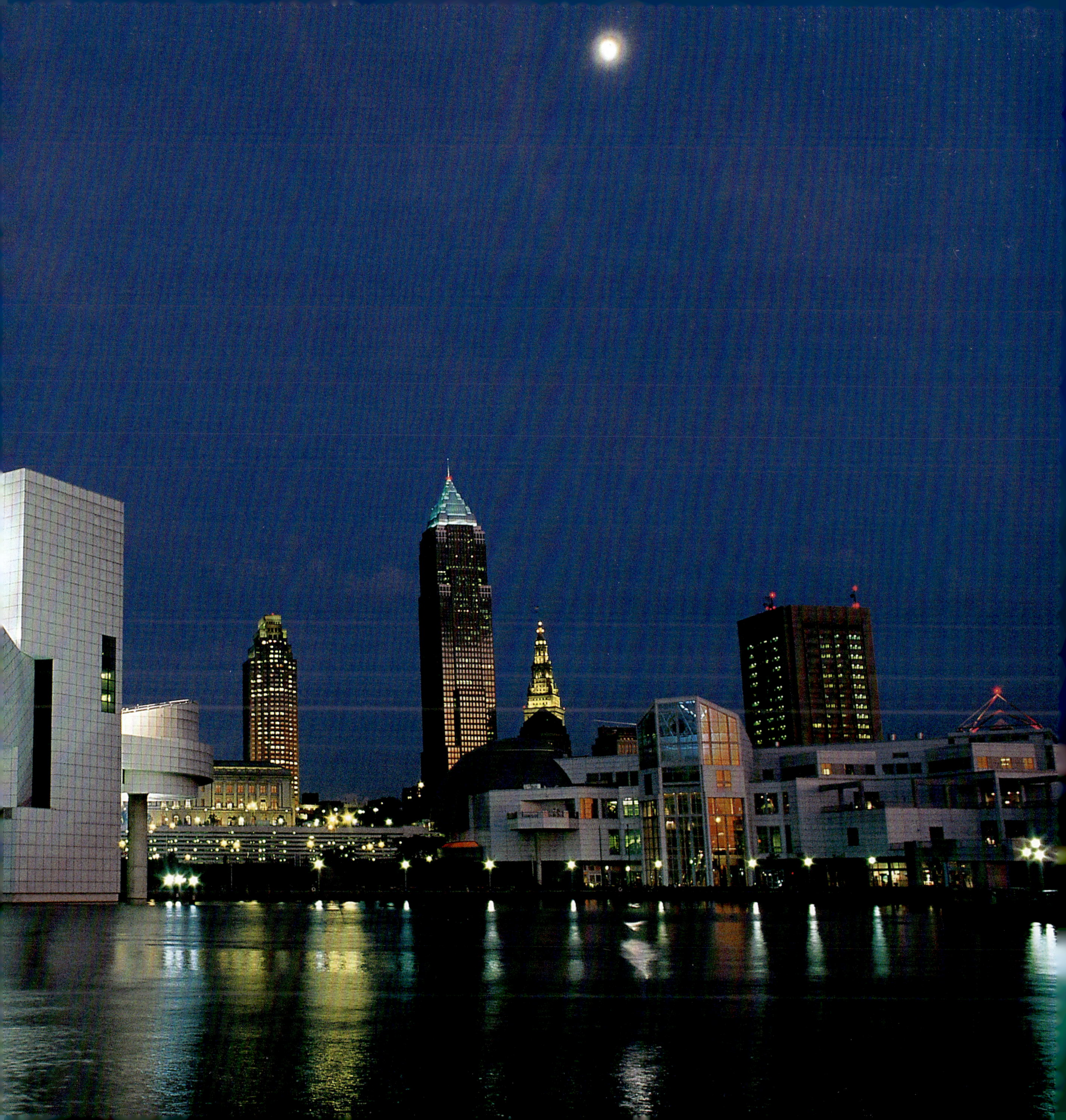

Cleveland has led the world in innovations. The first human blood transfusion was performed here in 1905 and the first electric traffic signal invented in 1914. Surgeons completed the world's first coronary artery bypass in the city in 1967.

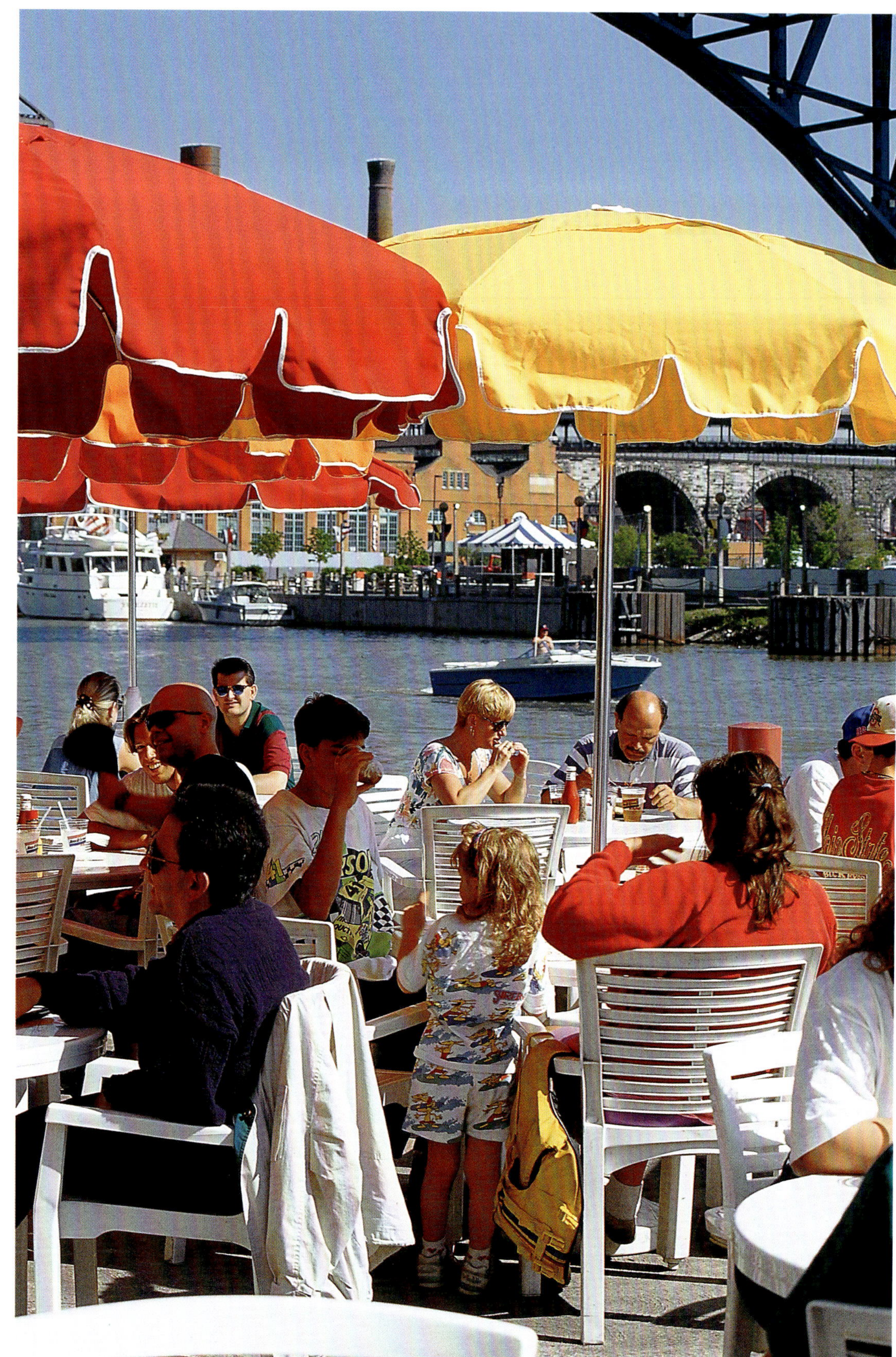

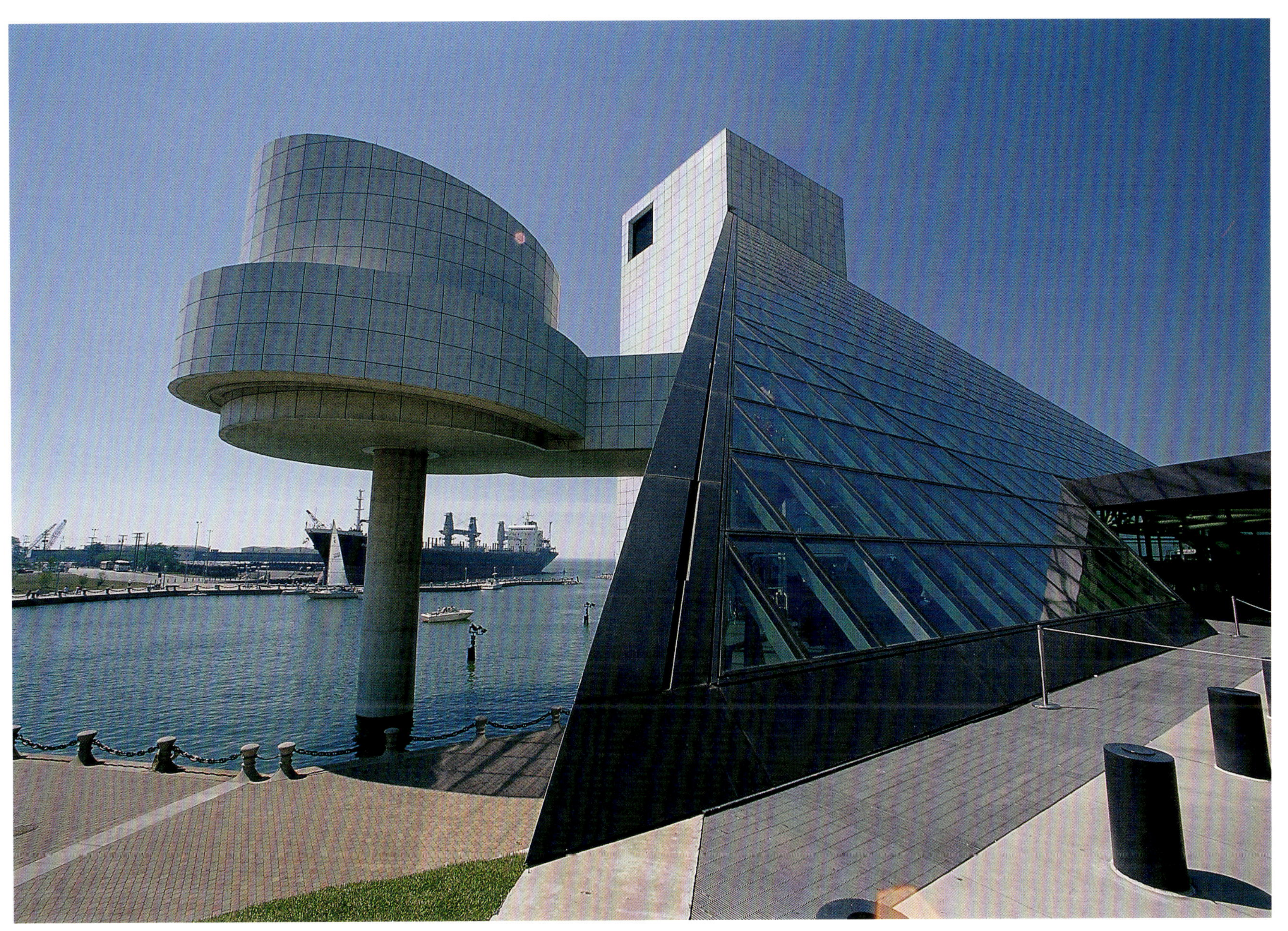

The Rock and Roll Hall of Fame and Museum in Cleveland celebrates the personalities behind American music. Inductees include performers, producers, and songwriters including John Lennon, Bob Dylan, Bruce Springsteen, and Elvis.

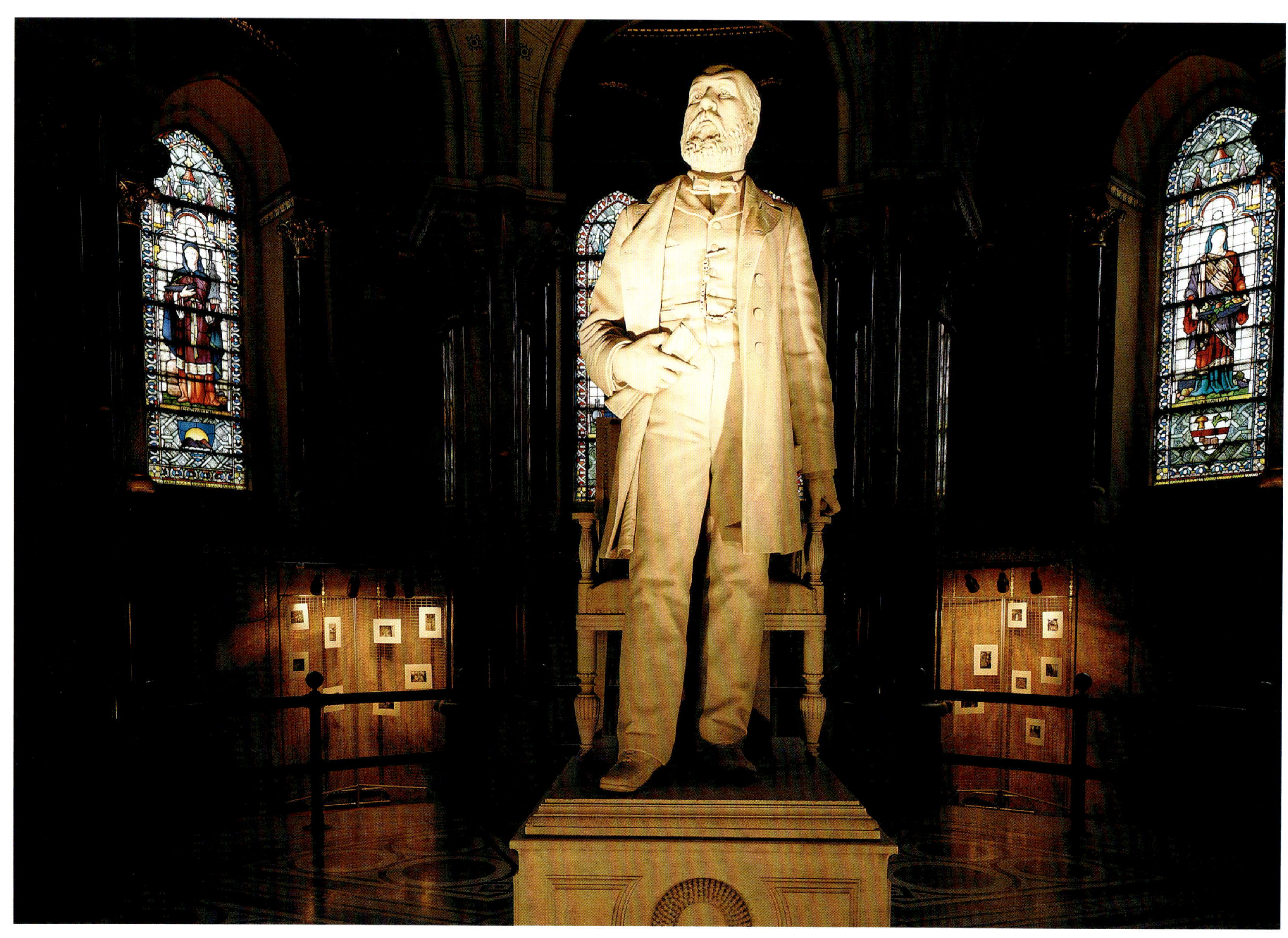

James A. Garfield National Historic Site was designated in 1980, almost 100 years after the twentieth president of the United States was shot by Charles Guiteau at the Baltimore and Potomac train station. Today's historic site preserves Garfield's family home.

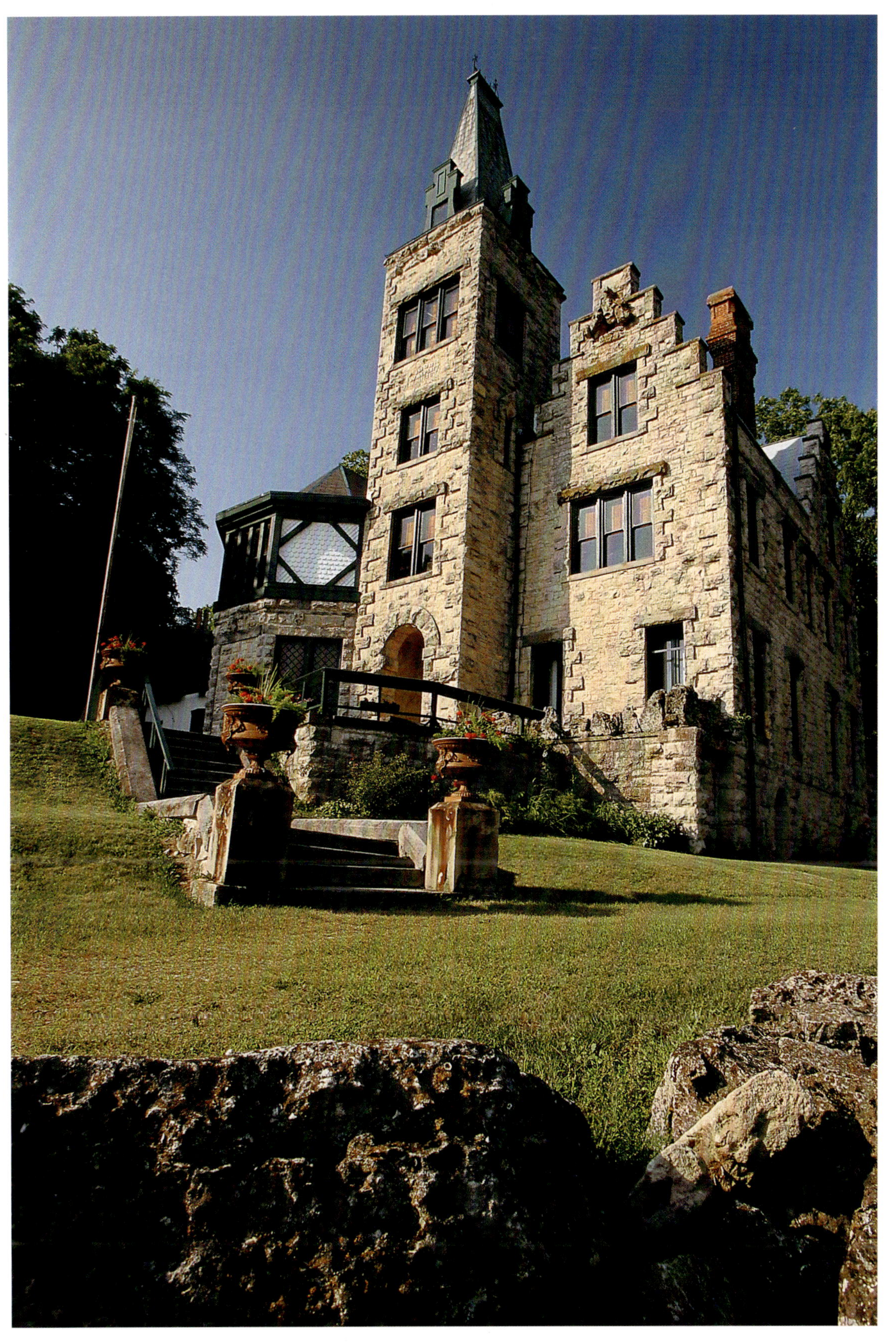

When Donn Piatt bought 500 acres of land during the Civil War, he envisioned Mac-O-Chee as a sprawling Swiss chalet, a gift for his wife. He abandoned the project after her death and his nephew, William McCoy Piatt, transformed the building into a Flemish château, filled with rare antiques and tapestries.

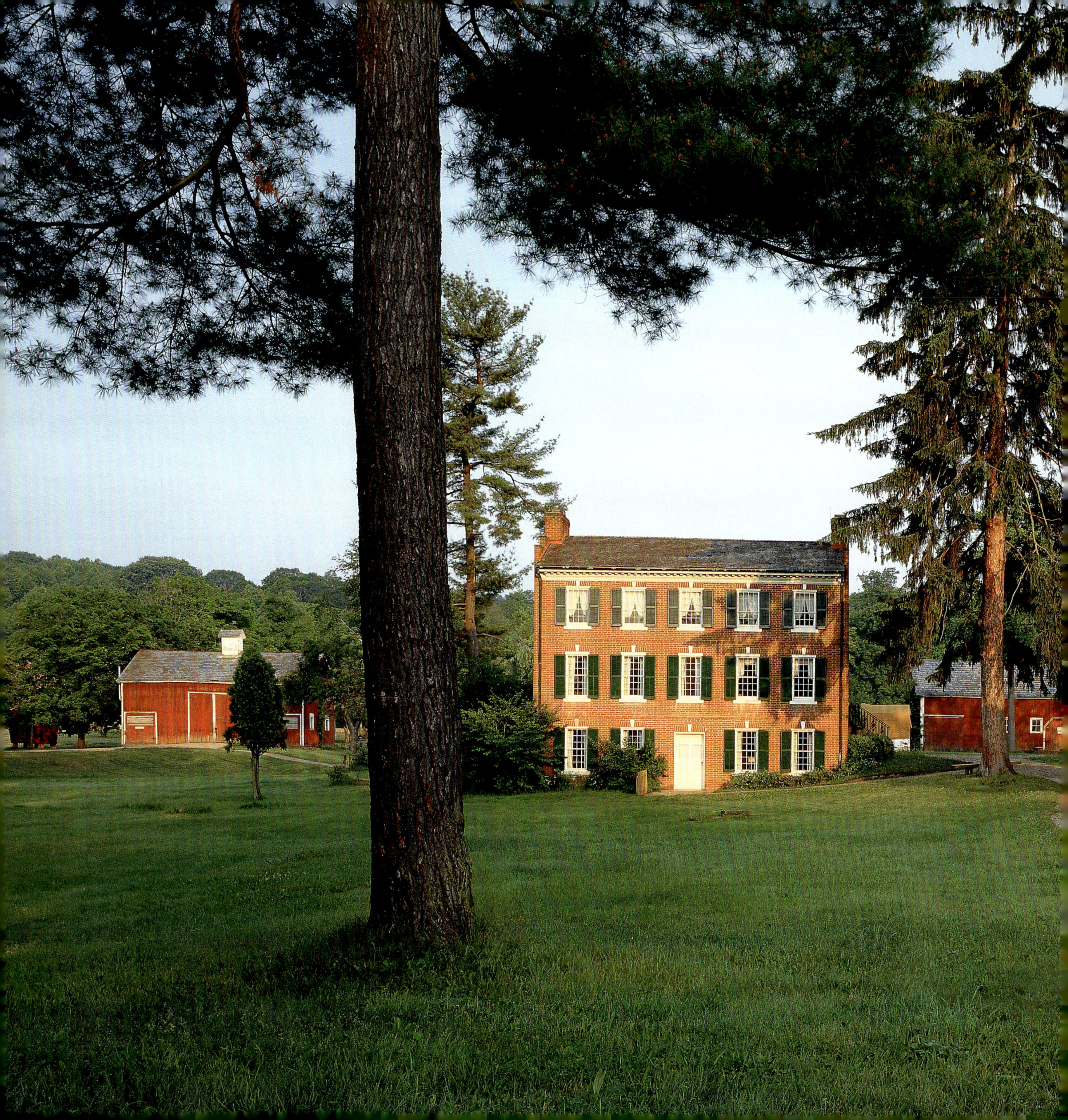

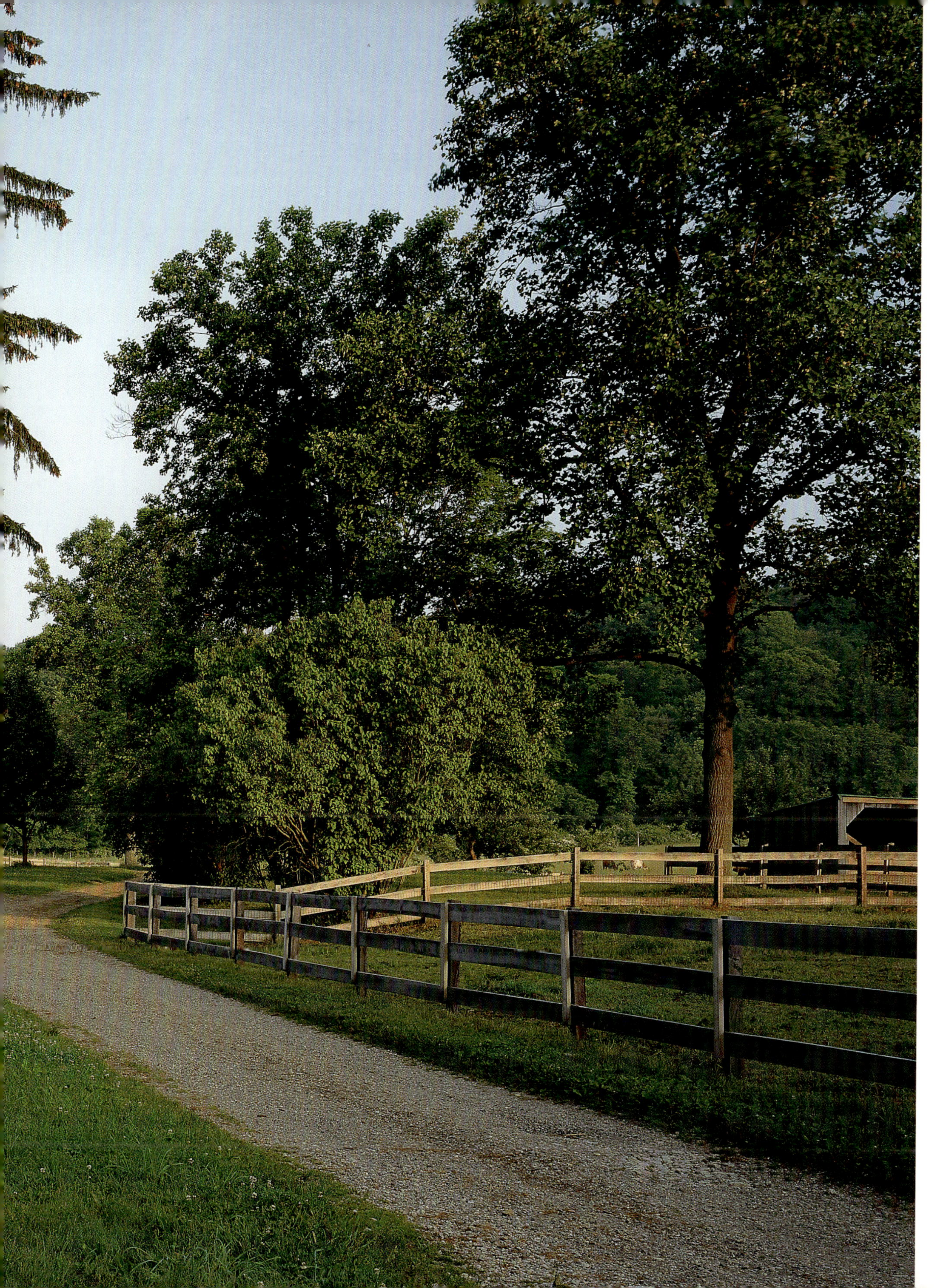

Jonathan Hale was one of the original settlers in the Cuyahoga River valley. Today, his 1850s homestead lets visitors capture life as it was more than a century ago. Costumed staff demonstrate woodworking, blacksmithing, and weaving.

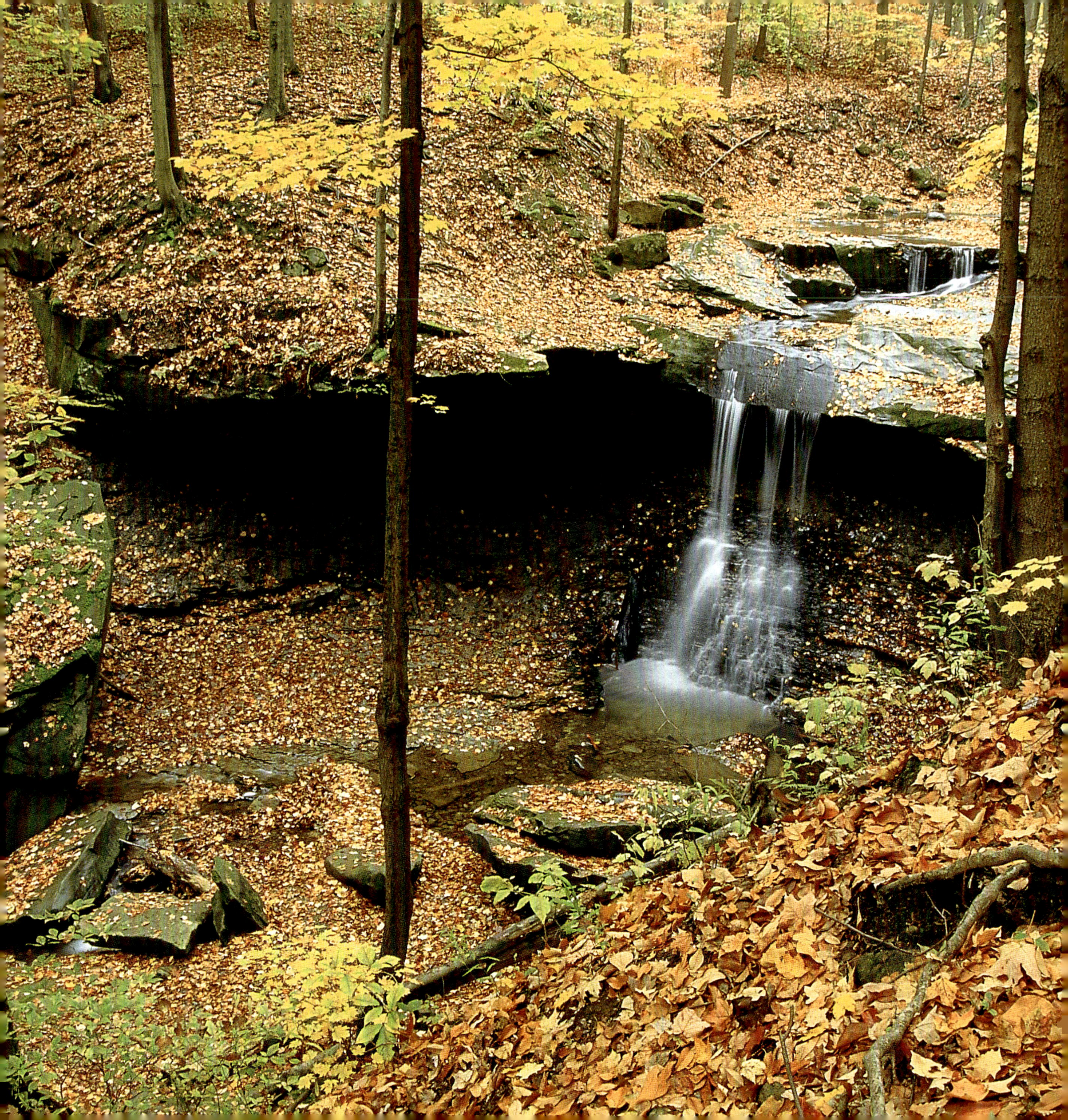

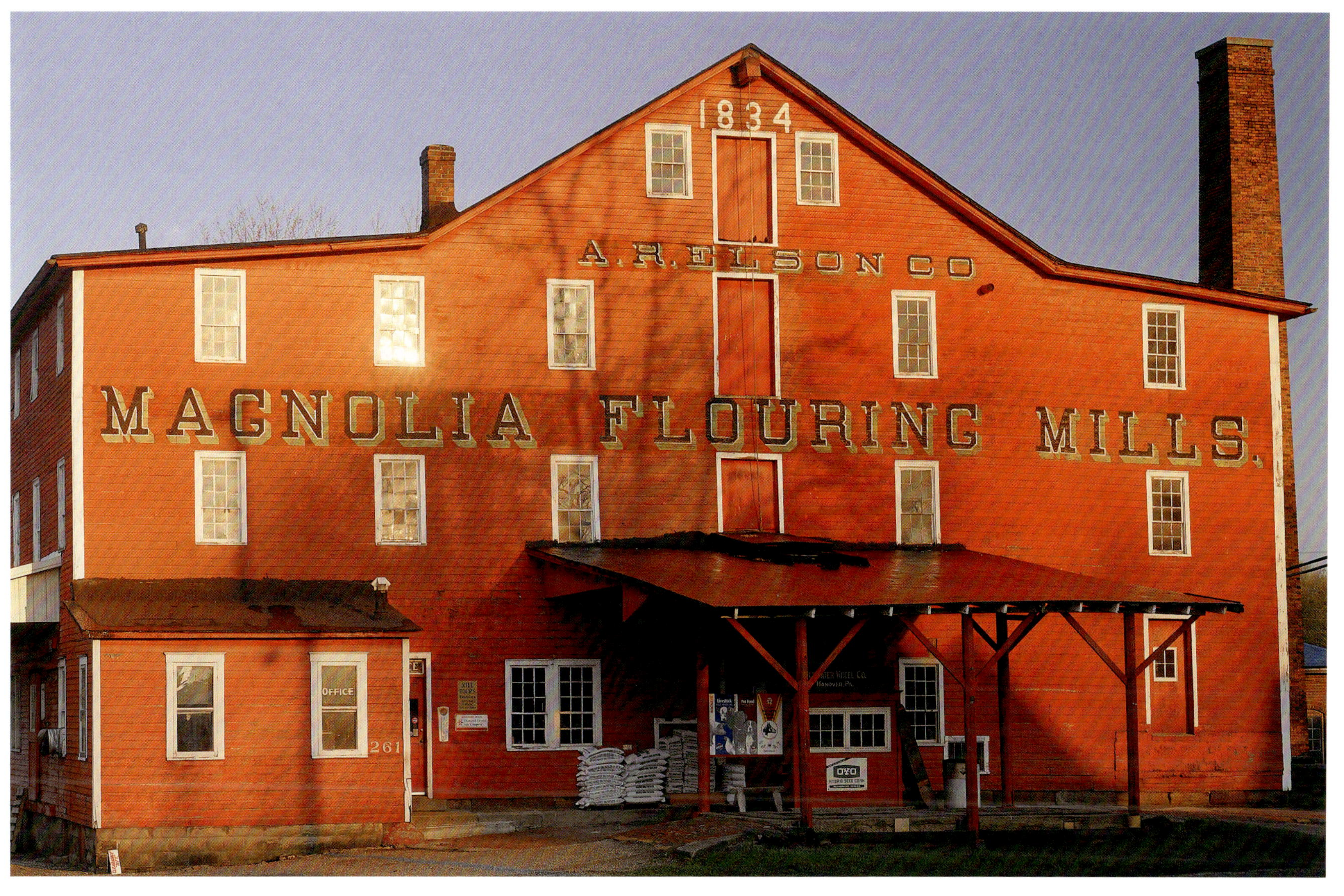

The oldest continuously operating mill in Ohio, the Magnolia Flouring Mill was built in 1834. Its success was ensured by the nearby railway and the presence of the Sandy and Beaver Canal, allowing easy transport of grain.

The Cuyahoga River is named for a native word — *Kaihohgha* — meaning crooked. From Cuyahoga Valley National Park, a 33,000-acre preserve designed to protect the valley, the river winds for 30 miles to Cleveland, where it flows into Lake Erie.

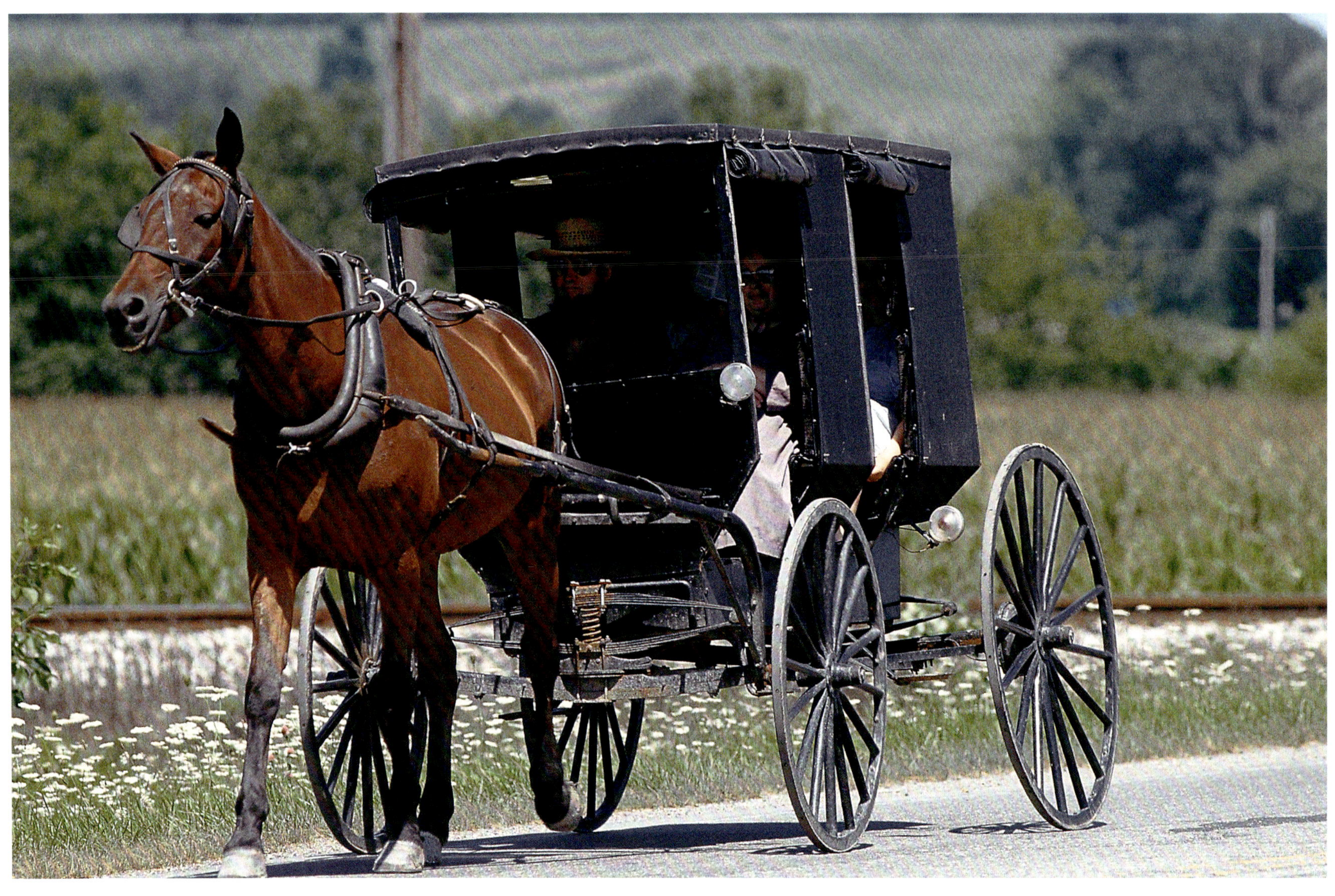

The Amish faith was born in Europe in the late 1600s, when Jacob Amman, originally a Mennonite, founded the sect. The community in Holmes County, Ohio, is the largest in the nation, but there are about 150,000 Amish people living in North America.

The Amish people of Ohio follow a faith that emphasizes humility, family, community, and independence from the world. To maintain this independence, the Amish wear traditional clothing and choose not to use electricity in their homes.

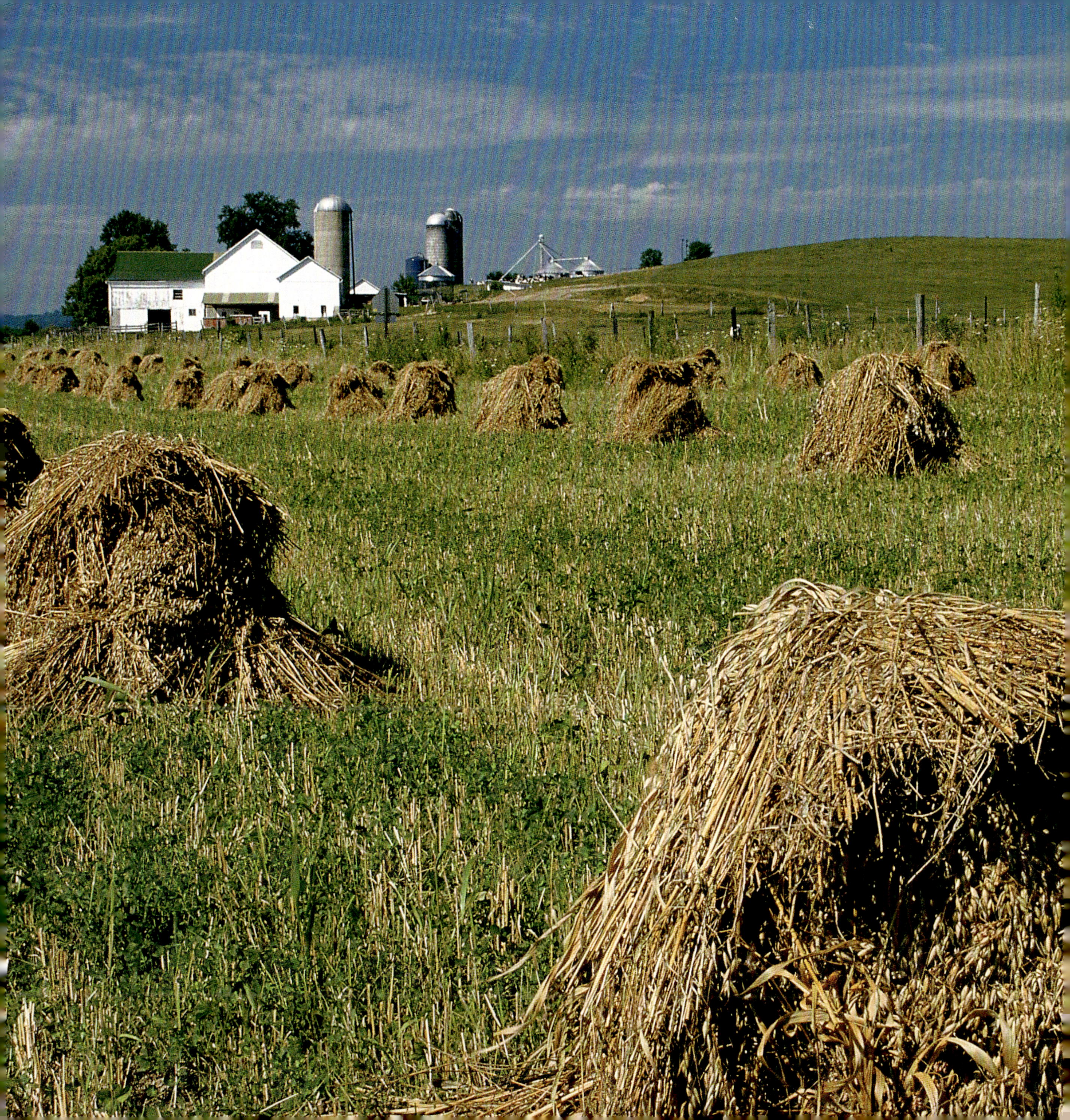

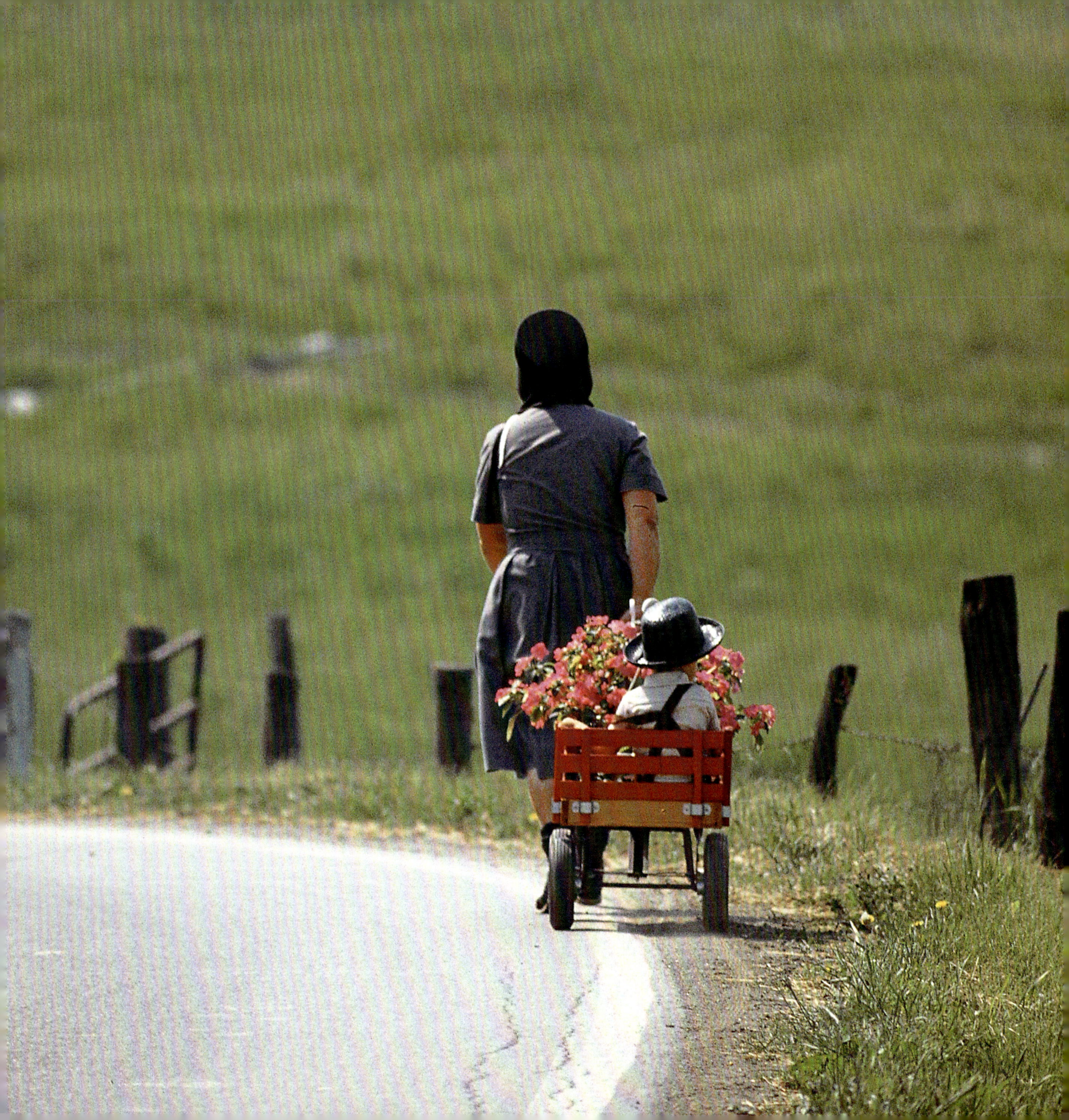

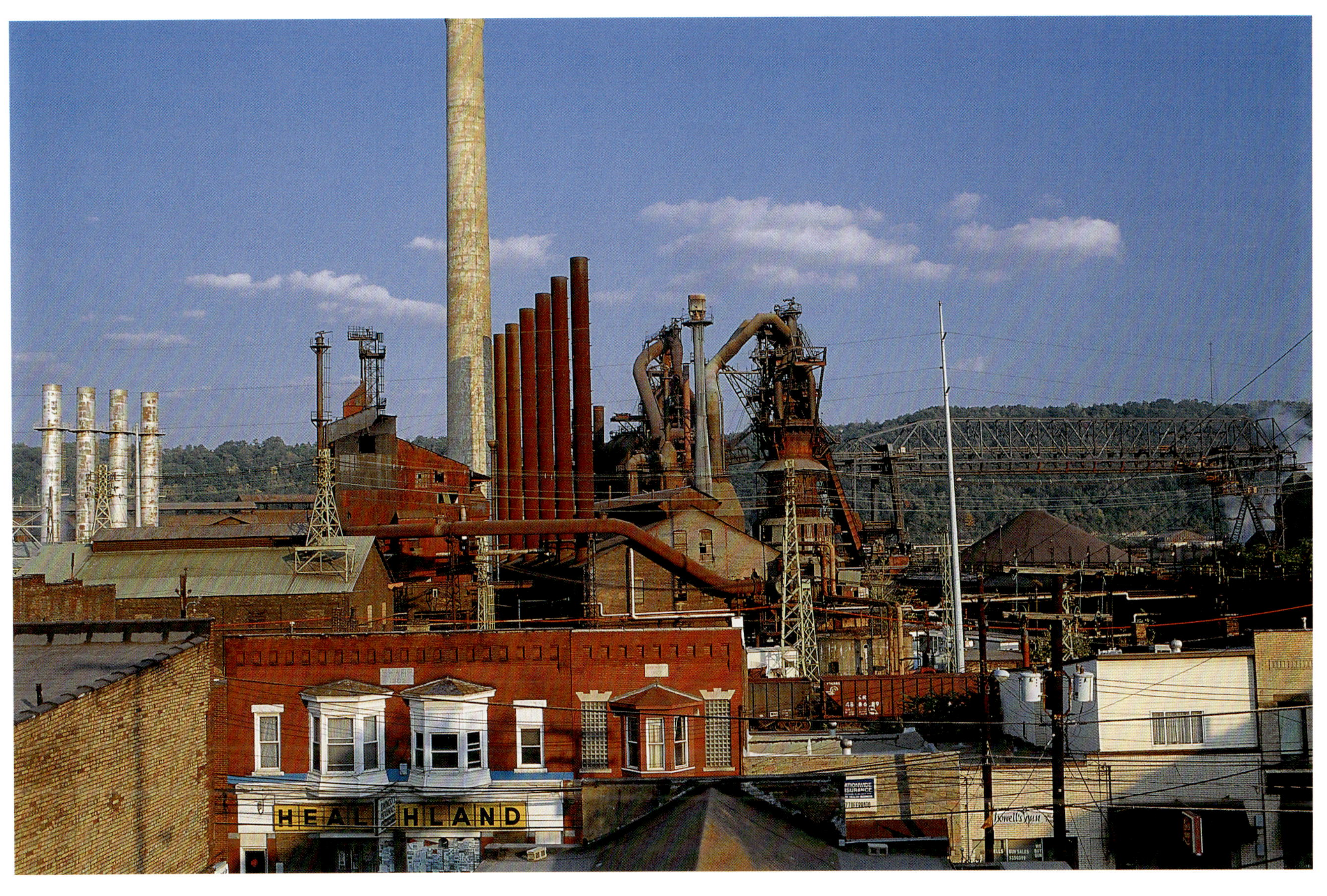

Mingo Junction in eastern Ohio is a town of just under 5,000 people. It has been home to a series of steel mills since the late 1800s, when Mingo Iron Works began production.

Most Amish children attend private schools until grade eight, when they begin work in family businesses or on local farms. Because their lifestyle is considered part of their religious beliefs, the U.S. Supreme Court has made an exception to laws that otherwise require children to attend high school.

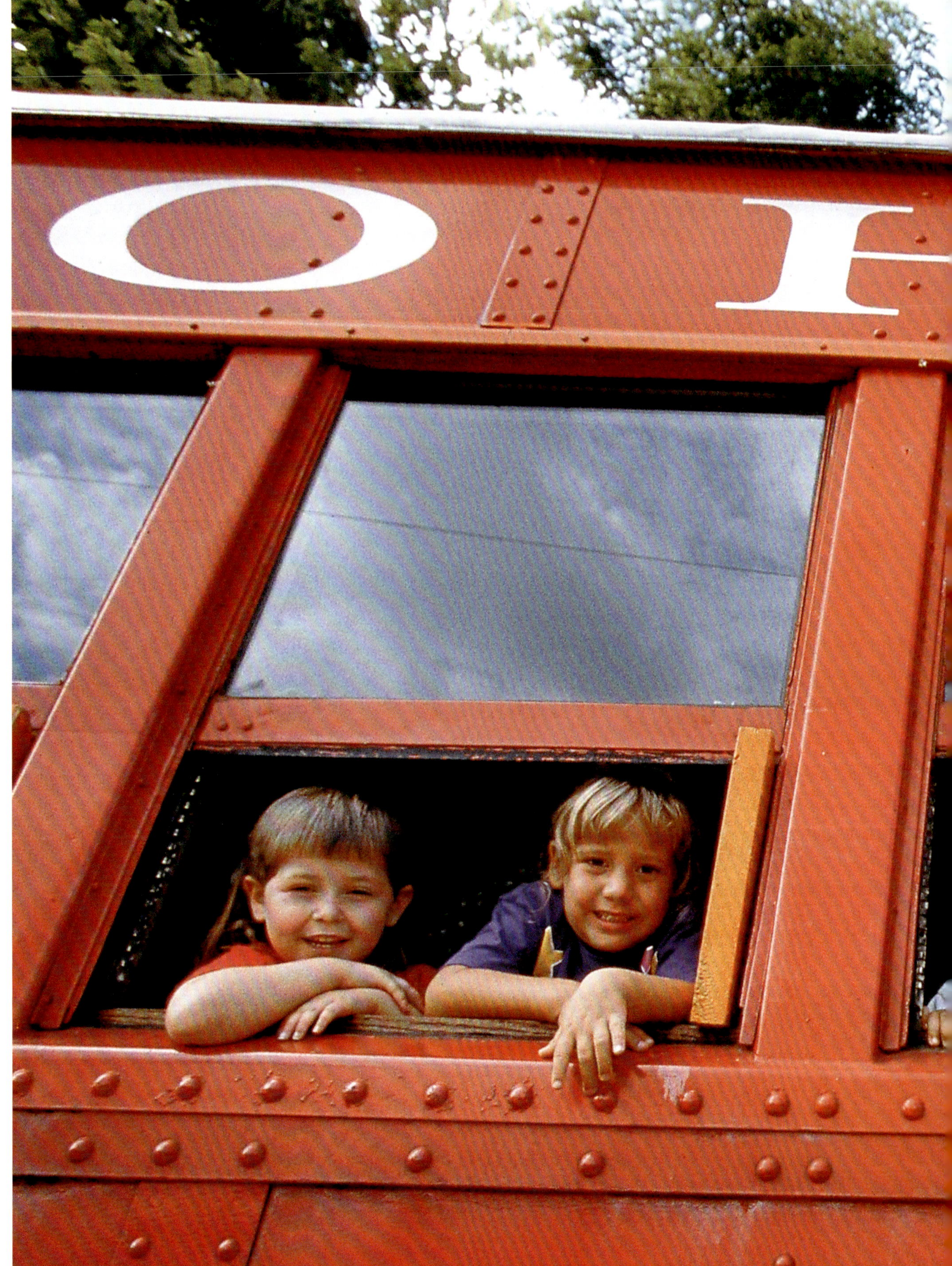

The Turtle Creek Valley Railway runs along tracks laid in 1880. The passenger cars that today carry sightseers through the rural beauty of the valley were built in the early 1900s.

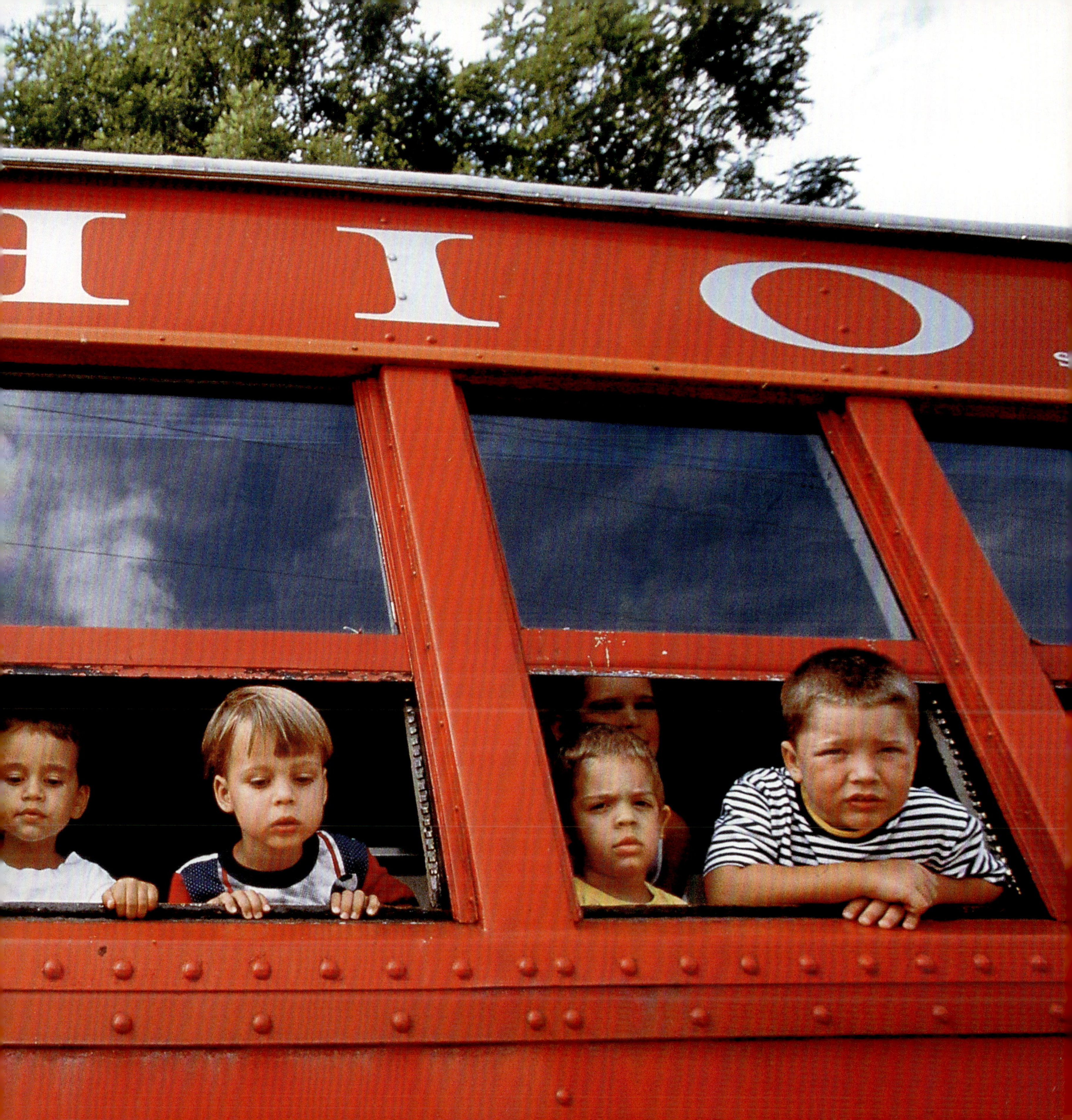

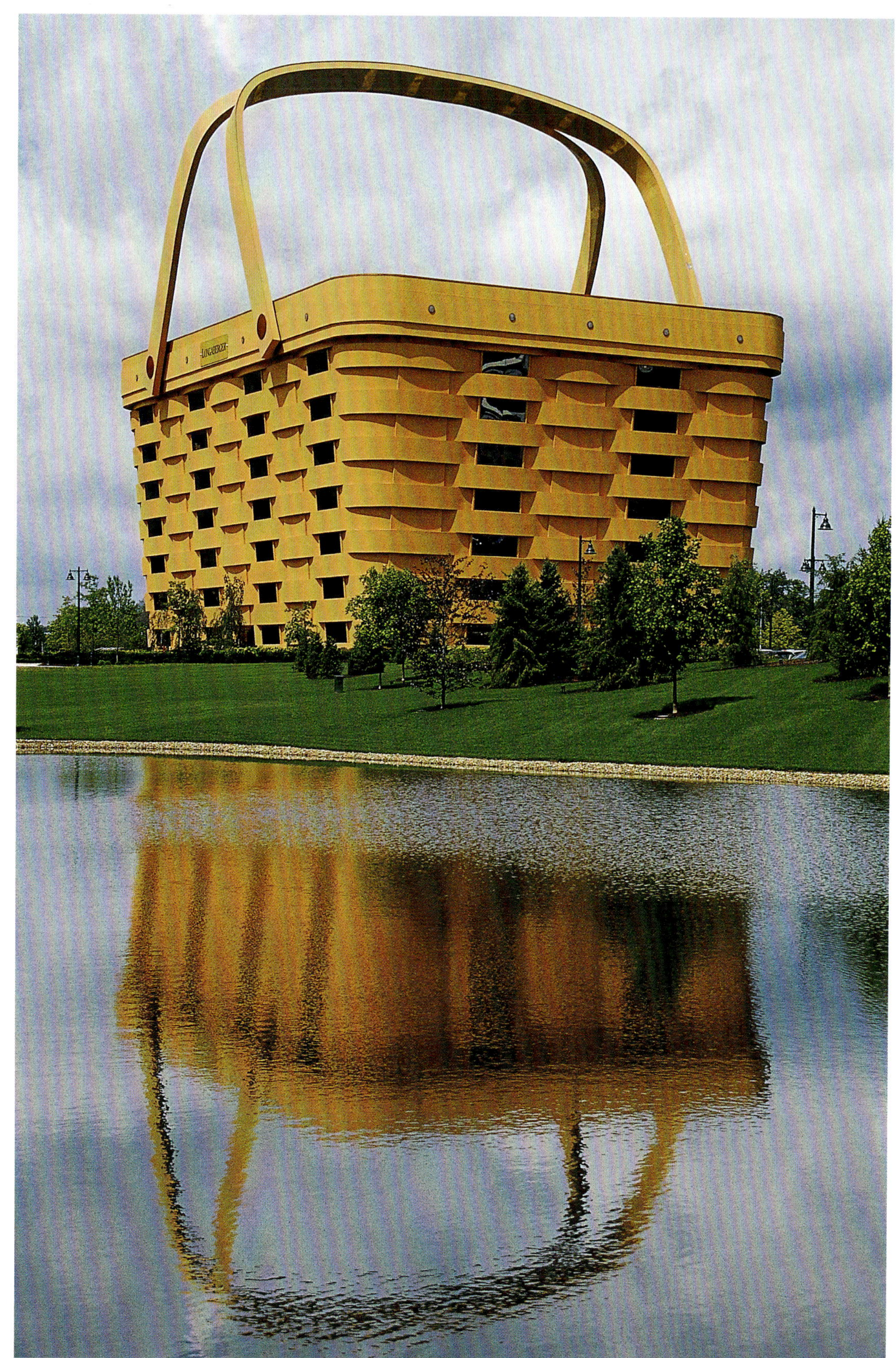

When the Longaberger Company planned their seven-story head offices in Newark, Ohio, they decided to stray from the usual office building design. Instead, they modeled the construction on one of their best-selling products — the Longaberger Medium Market Basket.

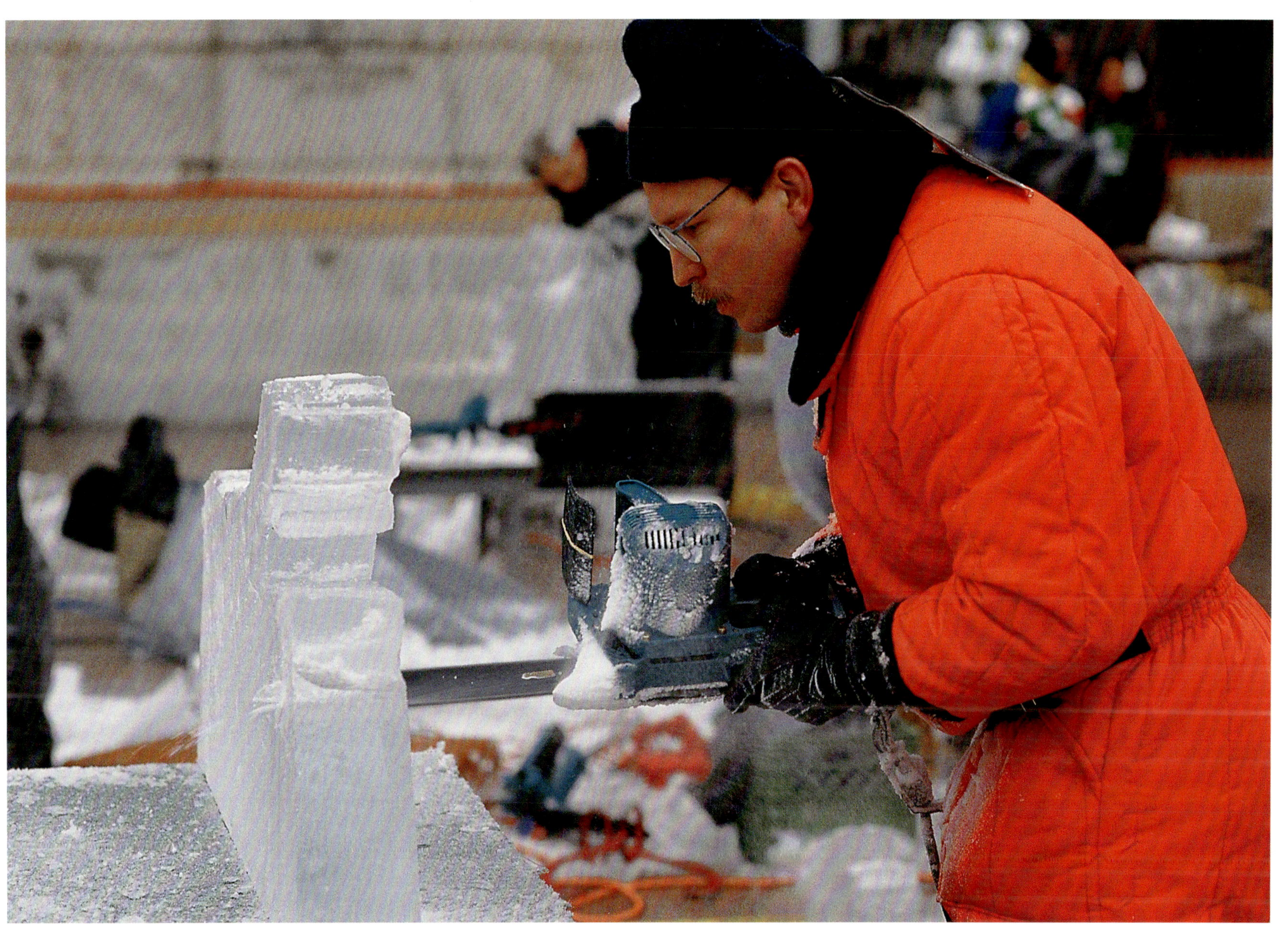

A chilly but determined artist completes his entry in an ice-sculpting contest in downtown Columbus. Fodor's Travel Publications has recently ranked the city as one of the most underrated places to visit in winter.

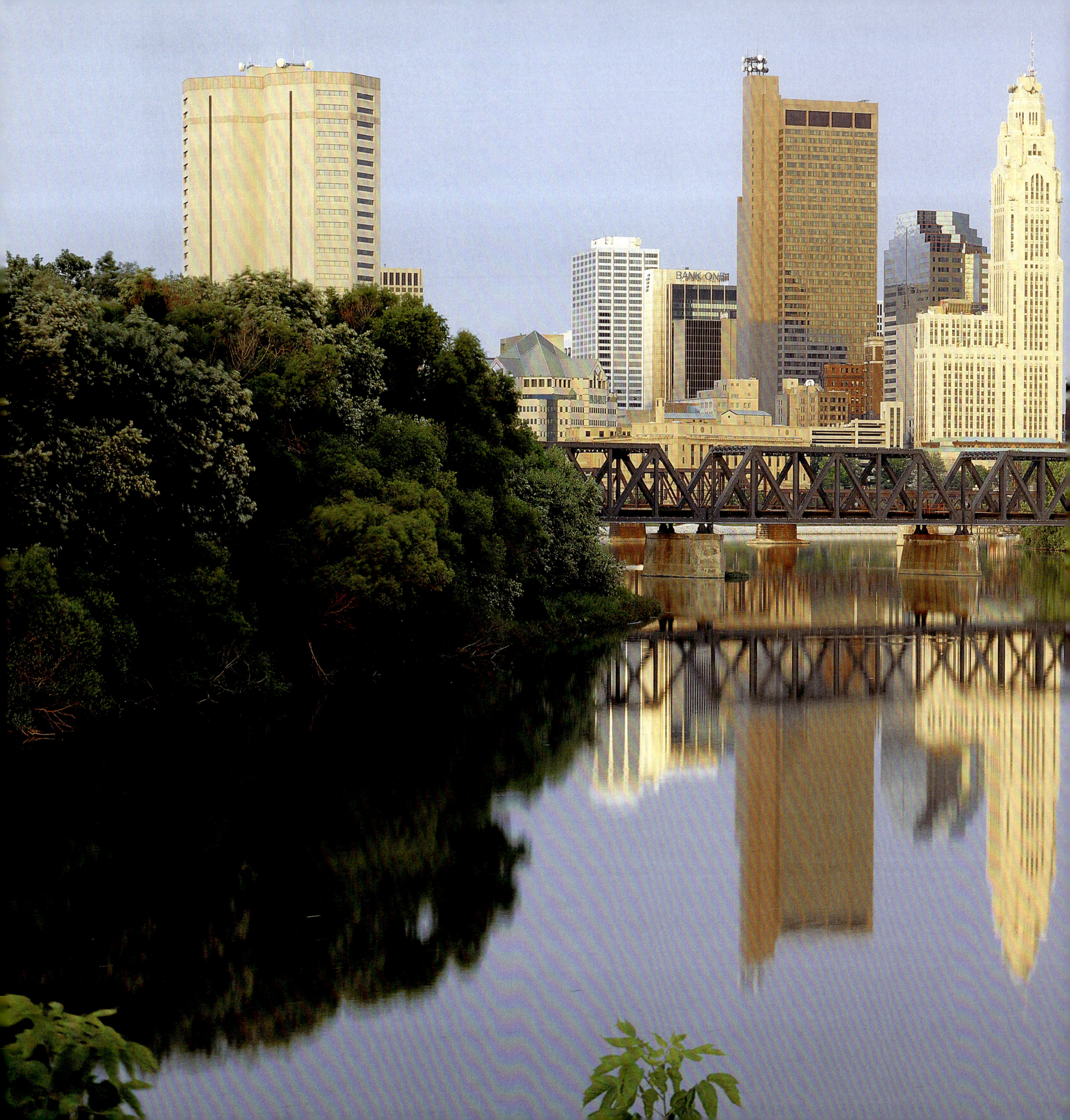
BANK ONE

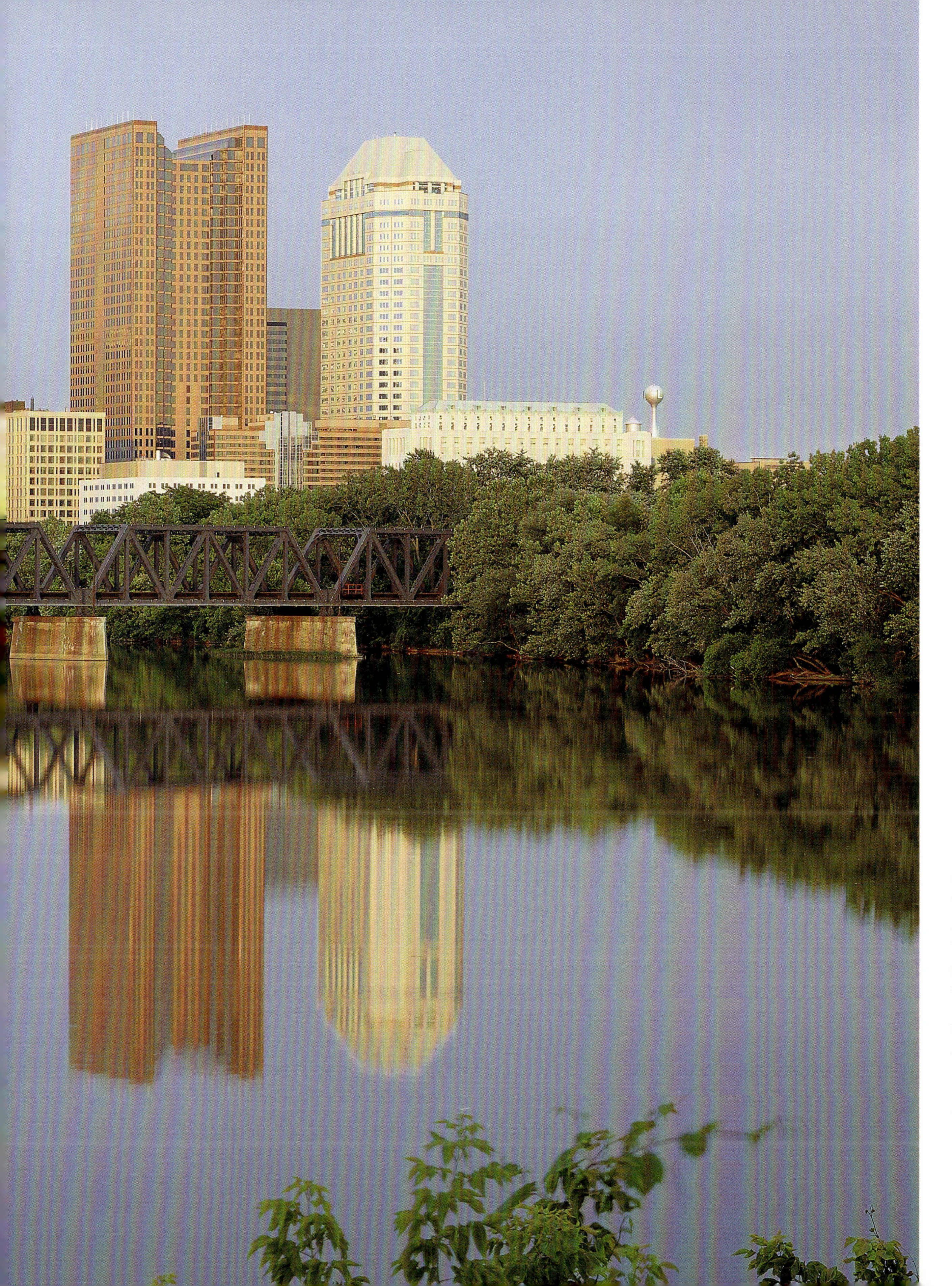

Columbus is quickly becoming one of the Midwest's largest centers for the arts. There are 20 theater companies, 18 museums, and more than 100 galleries within the city.

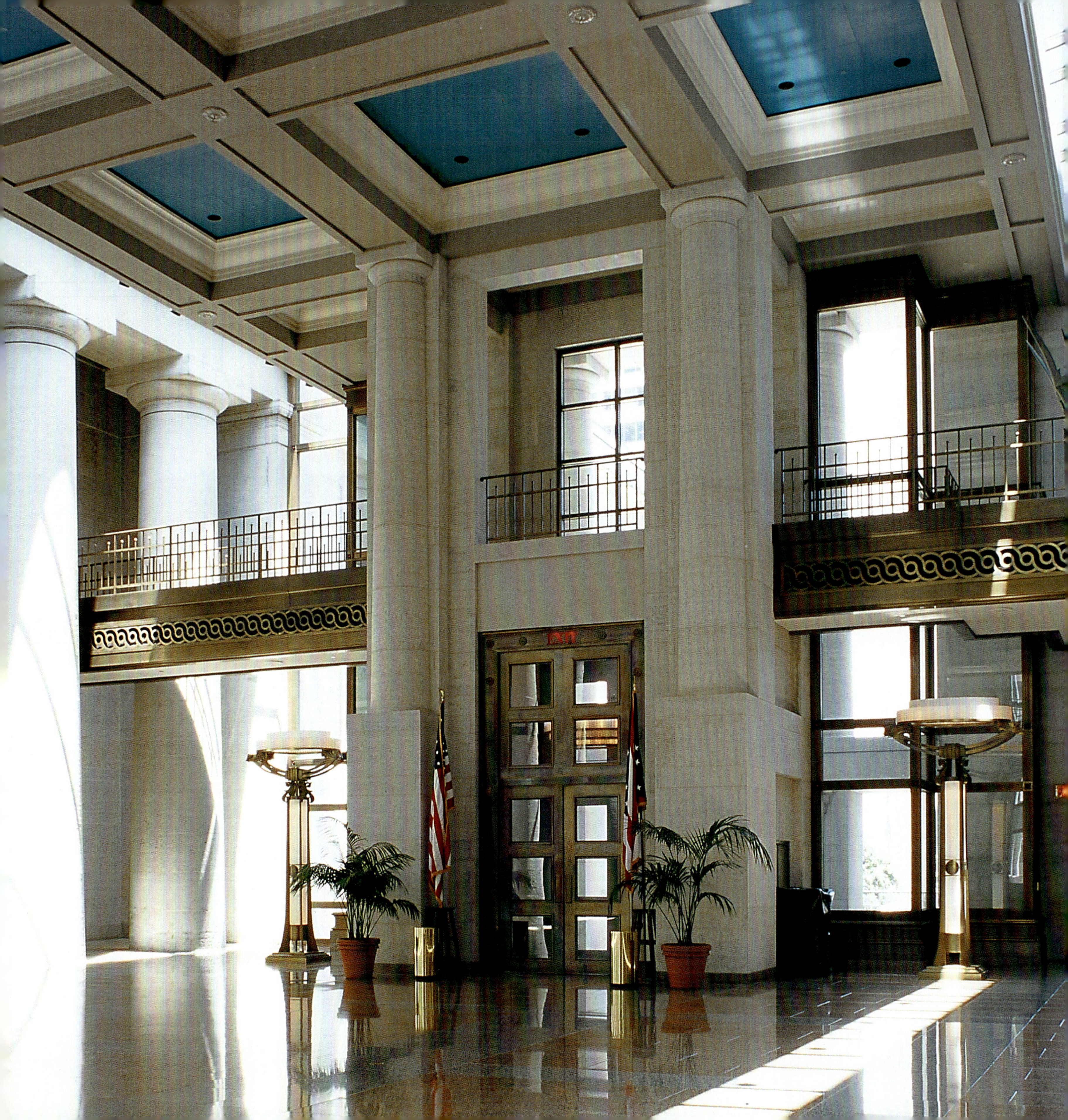

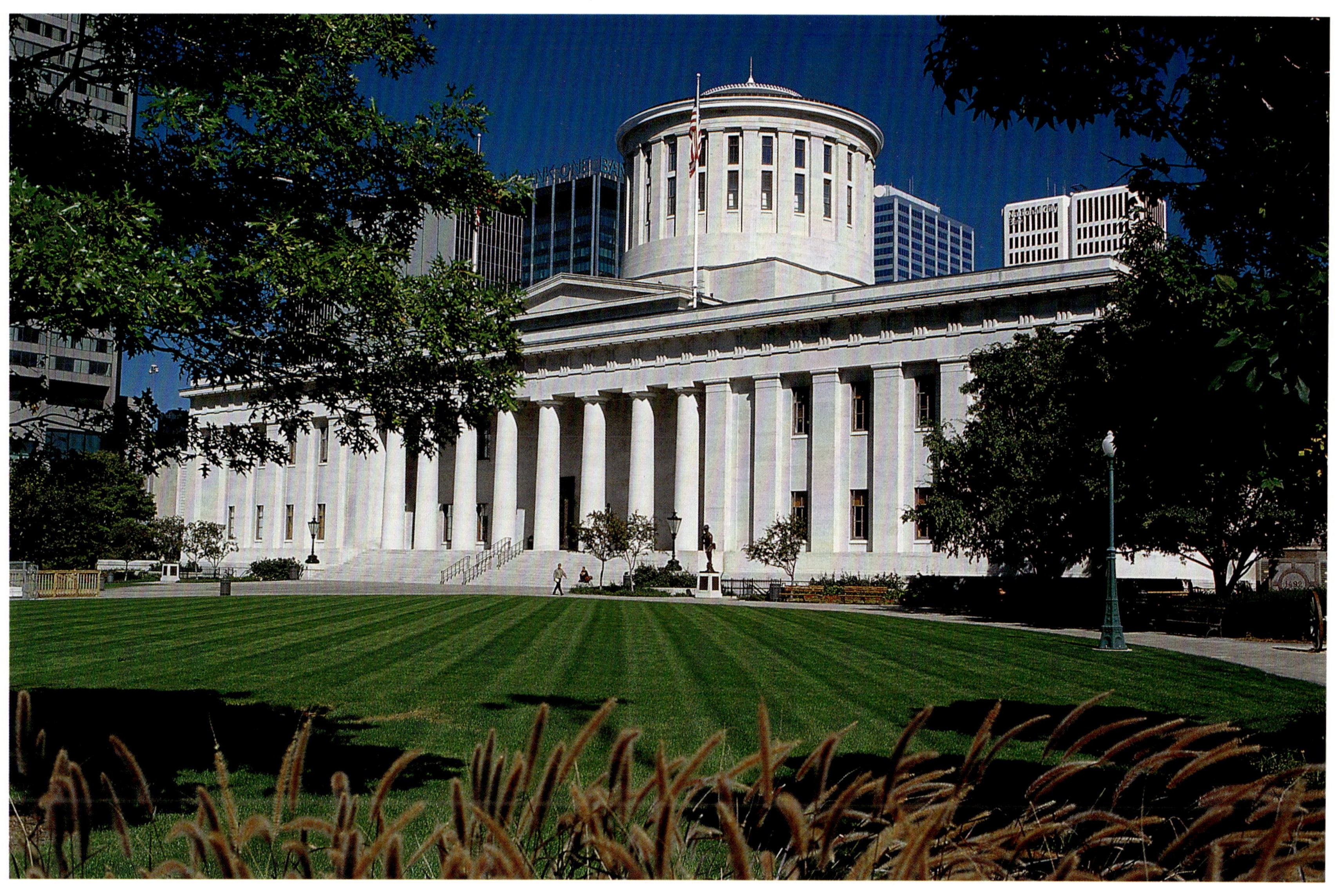

Built in the 1860s, Ohio's statehouse underwent numerous changes; eventually the original 53-room building had been divided into 317 rooms. In the early 1900s, the state restored the original architecture, complete with lofty ceilings, skylights, and decorative moldings.

A 29-foot-wide skylight crowns the rotunda of the State Capitol. More than 100 feet below, the floor consists of marble from around the world, including quarries in Vermont, Portugal, and Italy.

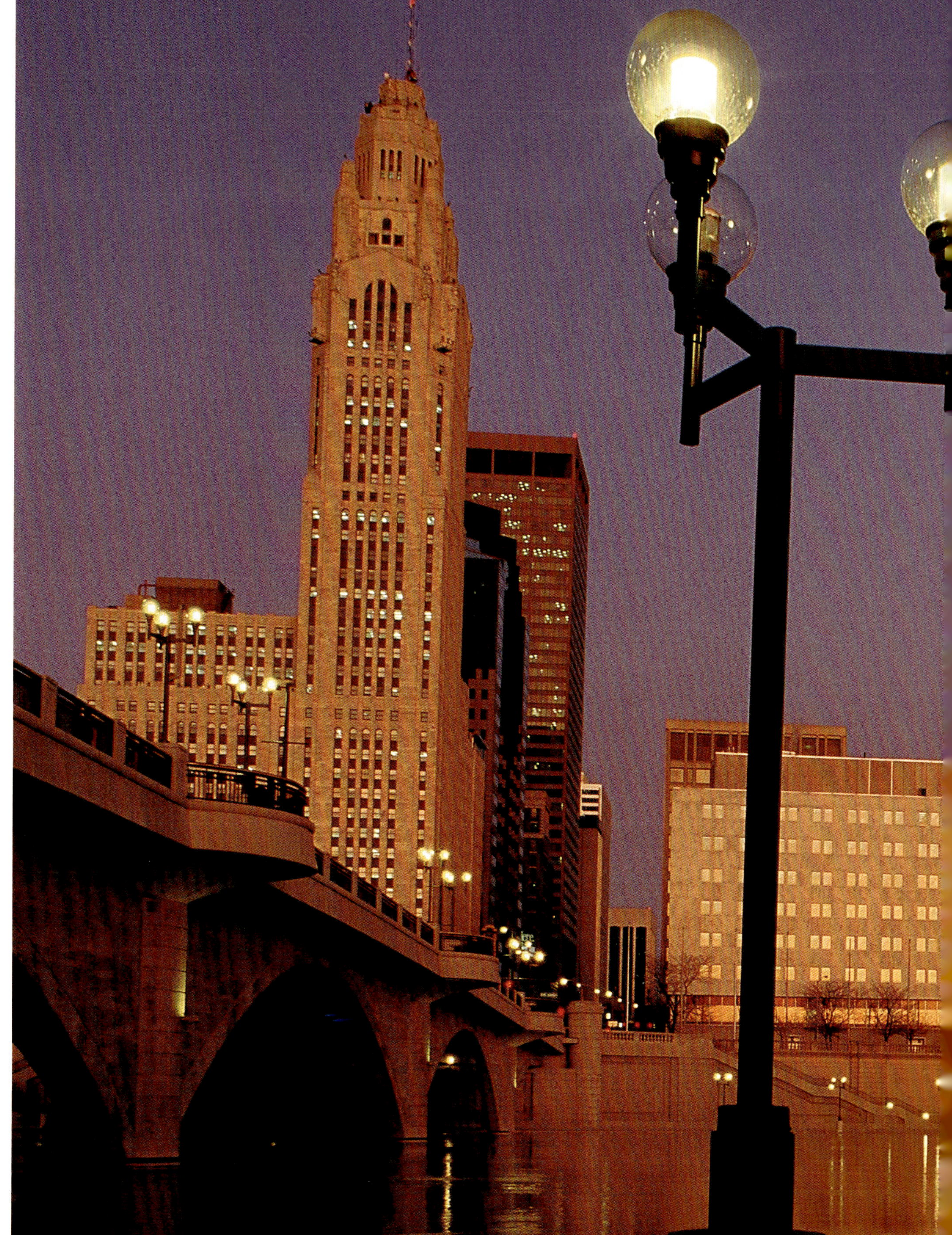

The largest city in the state and the fifteenth-largest in the nation, Columbus is a popular day trip for many. It's only 175 miles from Indianapolis, 189 from Pittsburgh, and 207 from Louisville. About 7 million guests each year stay overnight in the city.

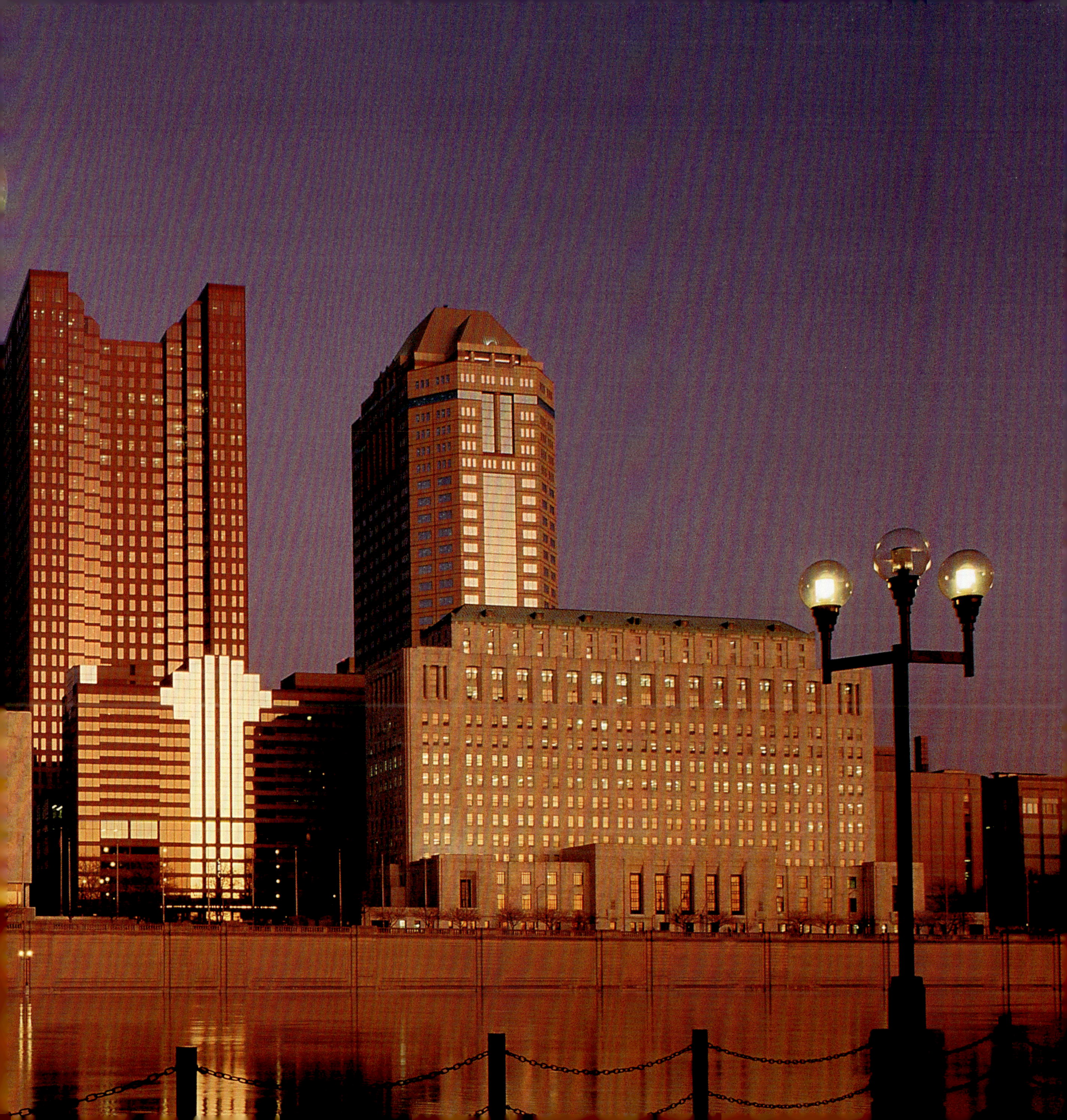

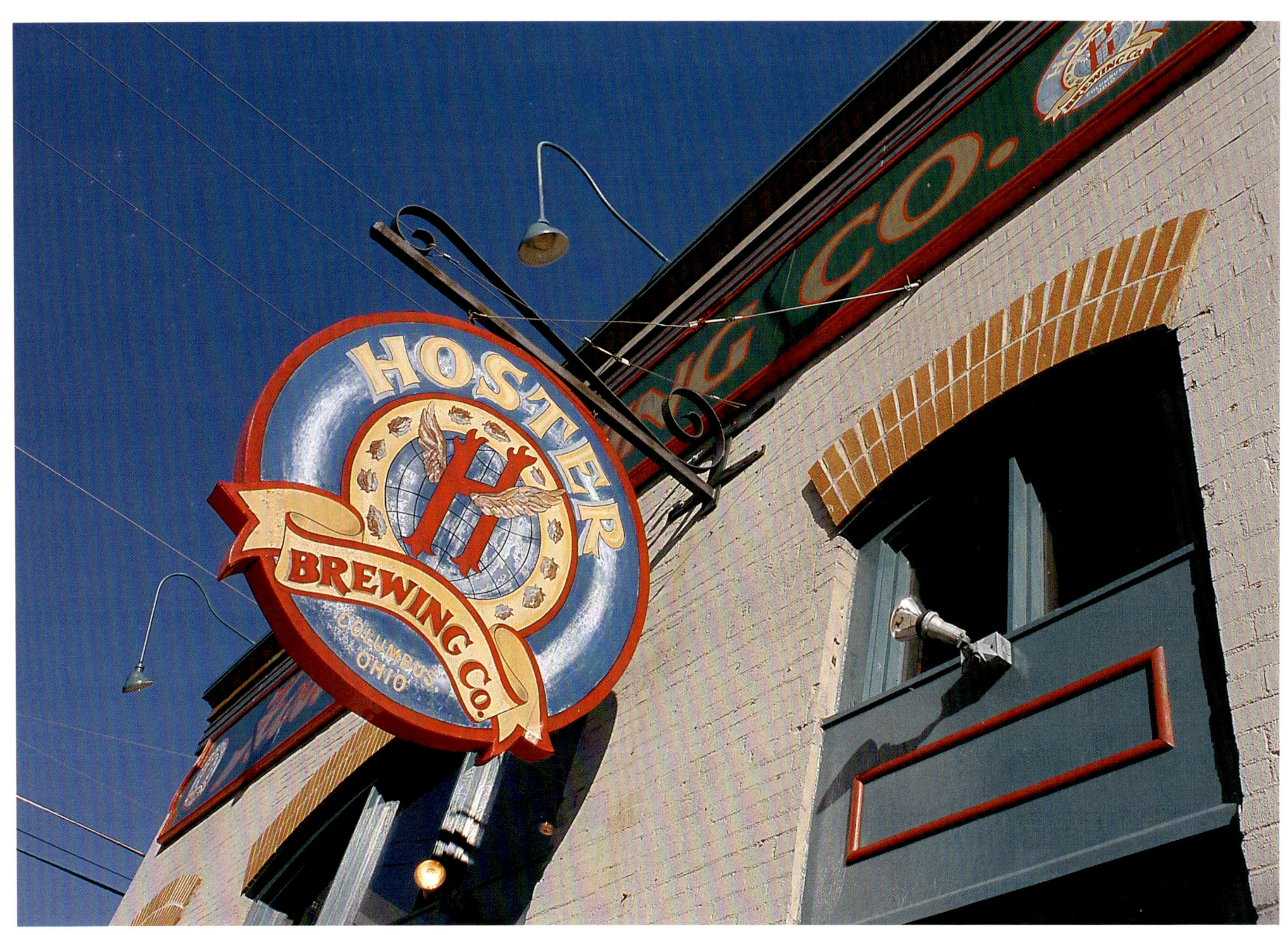

When Columbus residents and visitors are looking for nightlife, they head to the historic Brewery District, where micro-breweries open their doors to revelers, music drifts from the open windows of piano bars, and live entertainment beckons from every corner.

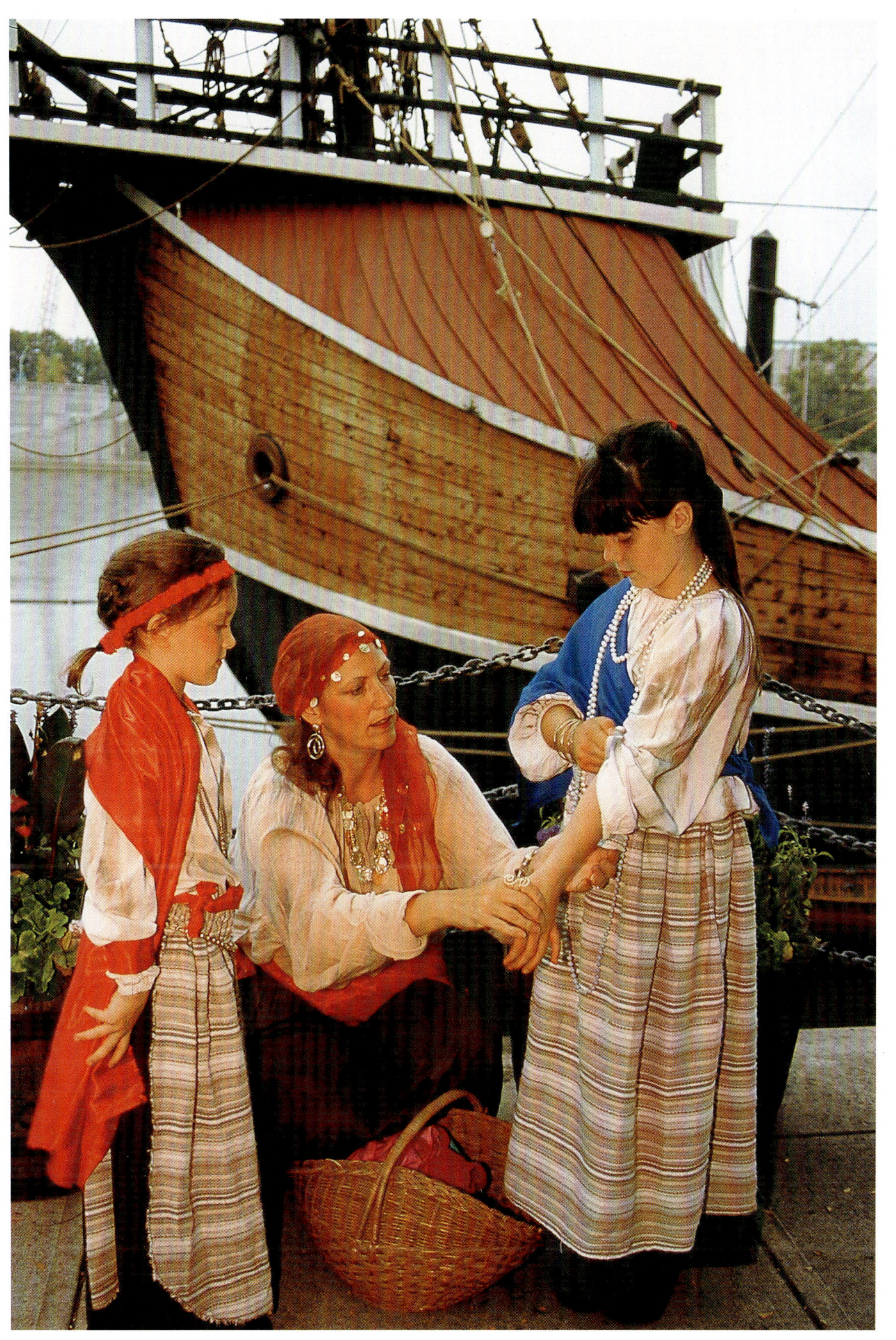

The shores of the Ohio River hold a surprise for visitors — a replica of Christopher Columbus' ship, the *Santa Maria*. The 98-foot-long vessel is the venue for an annual musical production that chronicles the explorer's arrival in America.

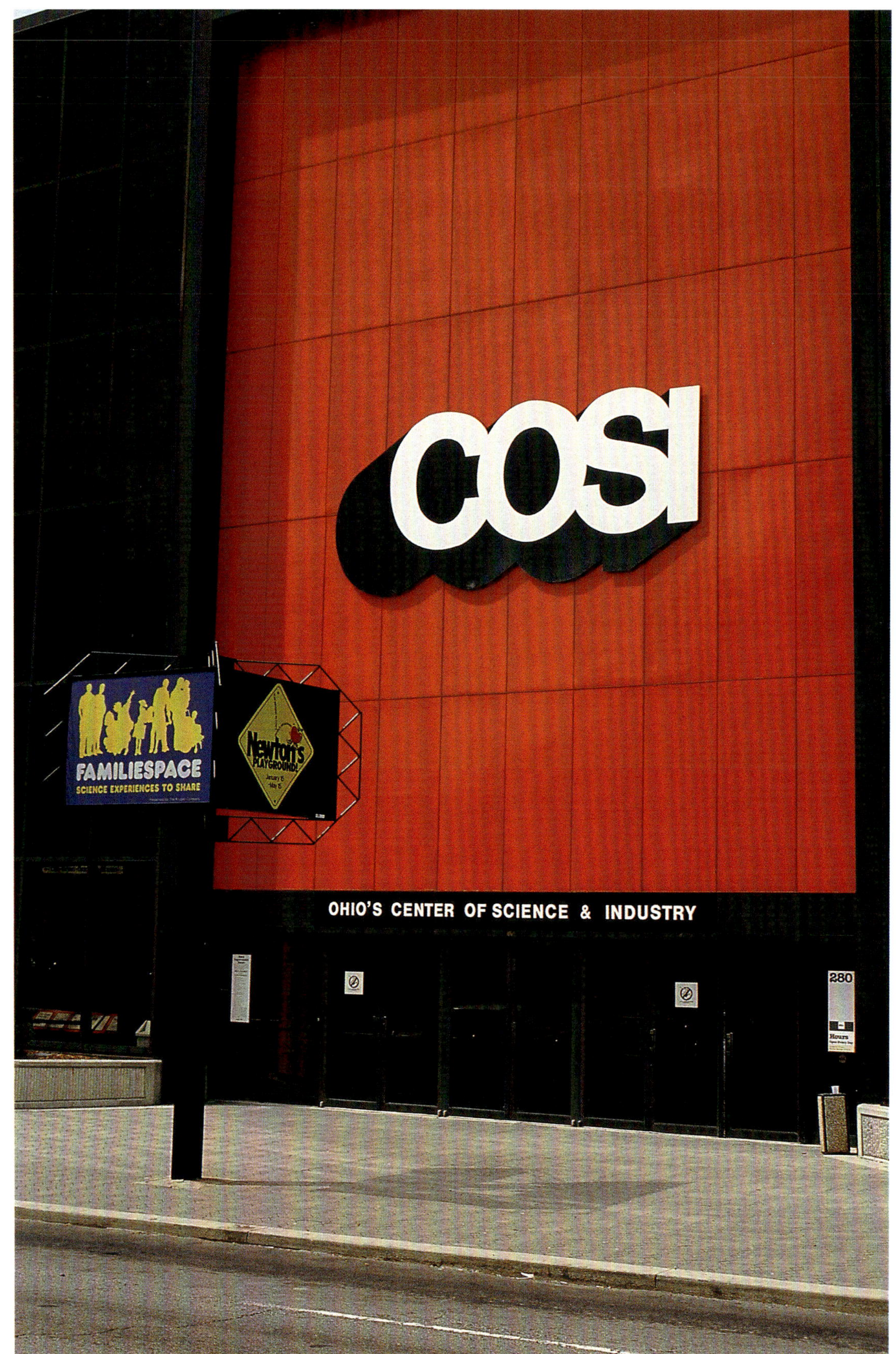

The Center of Science and Industry, or COSI, is known as the Fascination Destination and houses a collection of displays and exhibits designed to inspire. The renowned science center has attracted more than 16 million visitors since it opened in Columbus in 1964.

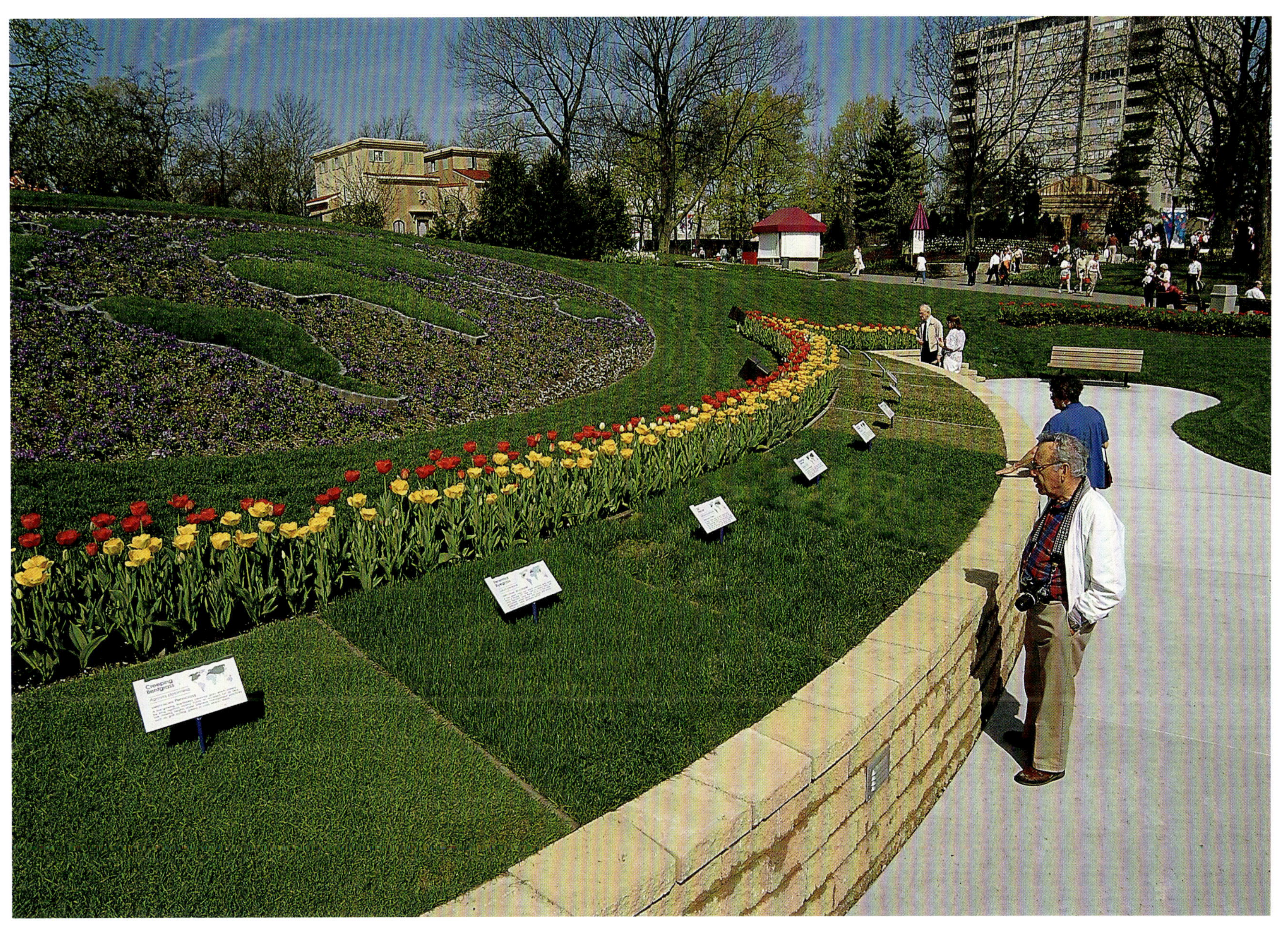

As well as a conservatory, Franklin Park offers five acres of formally landscaped grounds, sculptures and various theme gardens, such as a Japanese Garden and a Victory Garden.

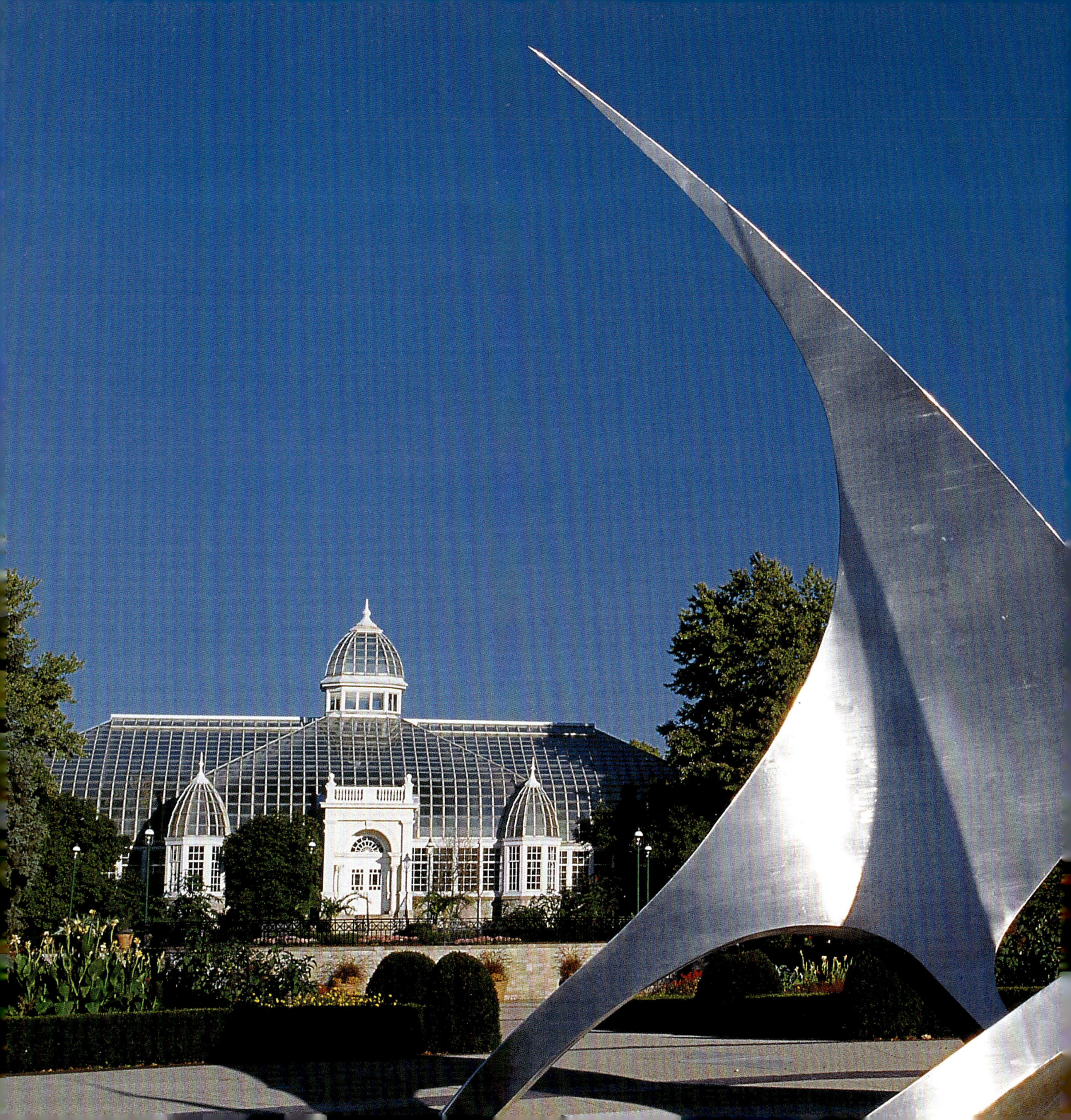

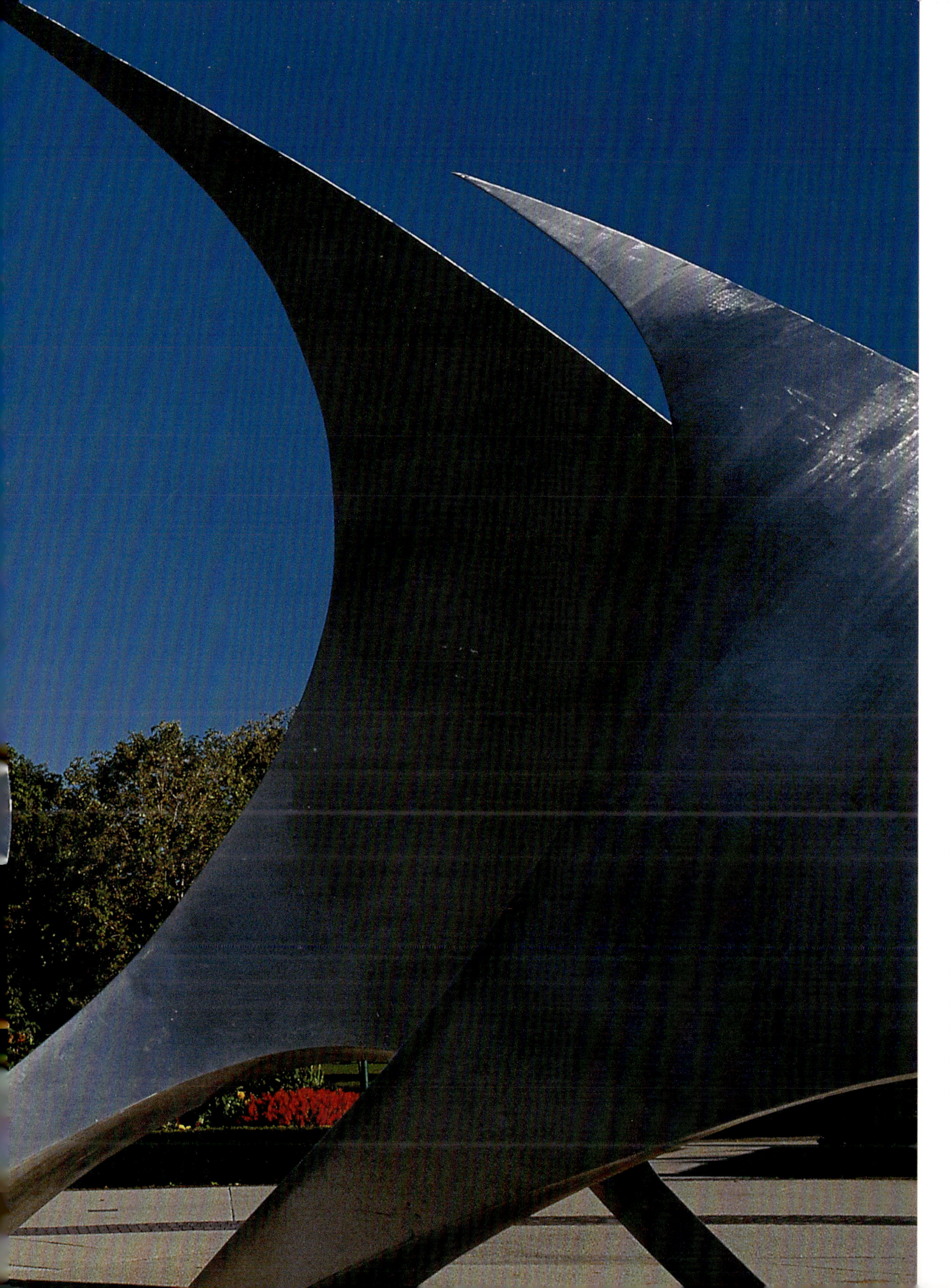

Nine climates under one roof allow Franklin Park visitors to wander from the tropics to the desert. Built in 1859 and repeatedly expanded, the conservatory echoes the style of London's famous Crystal Palace.

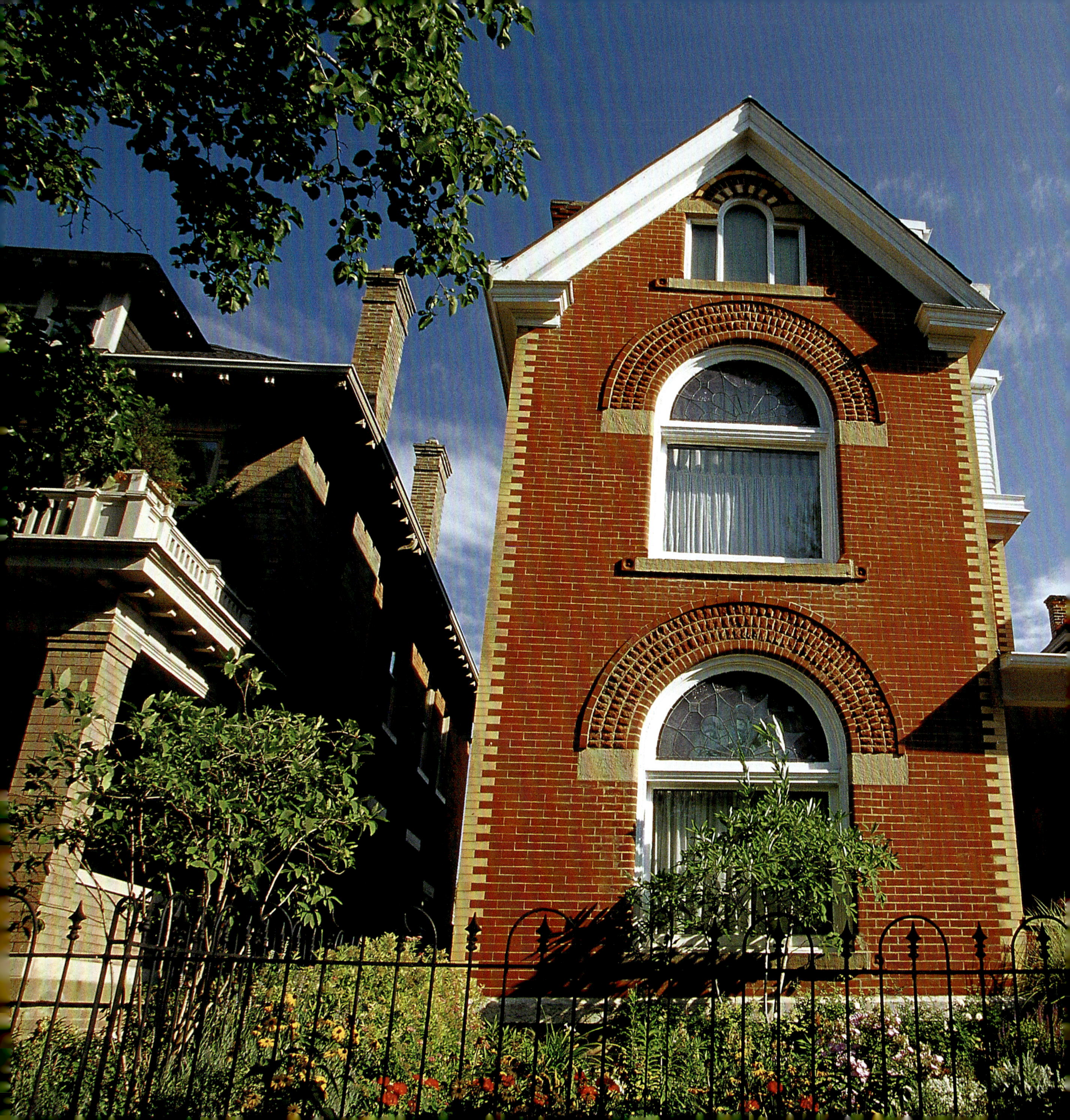

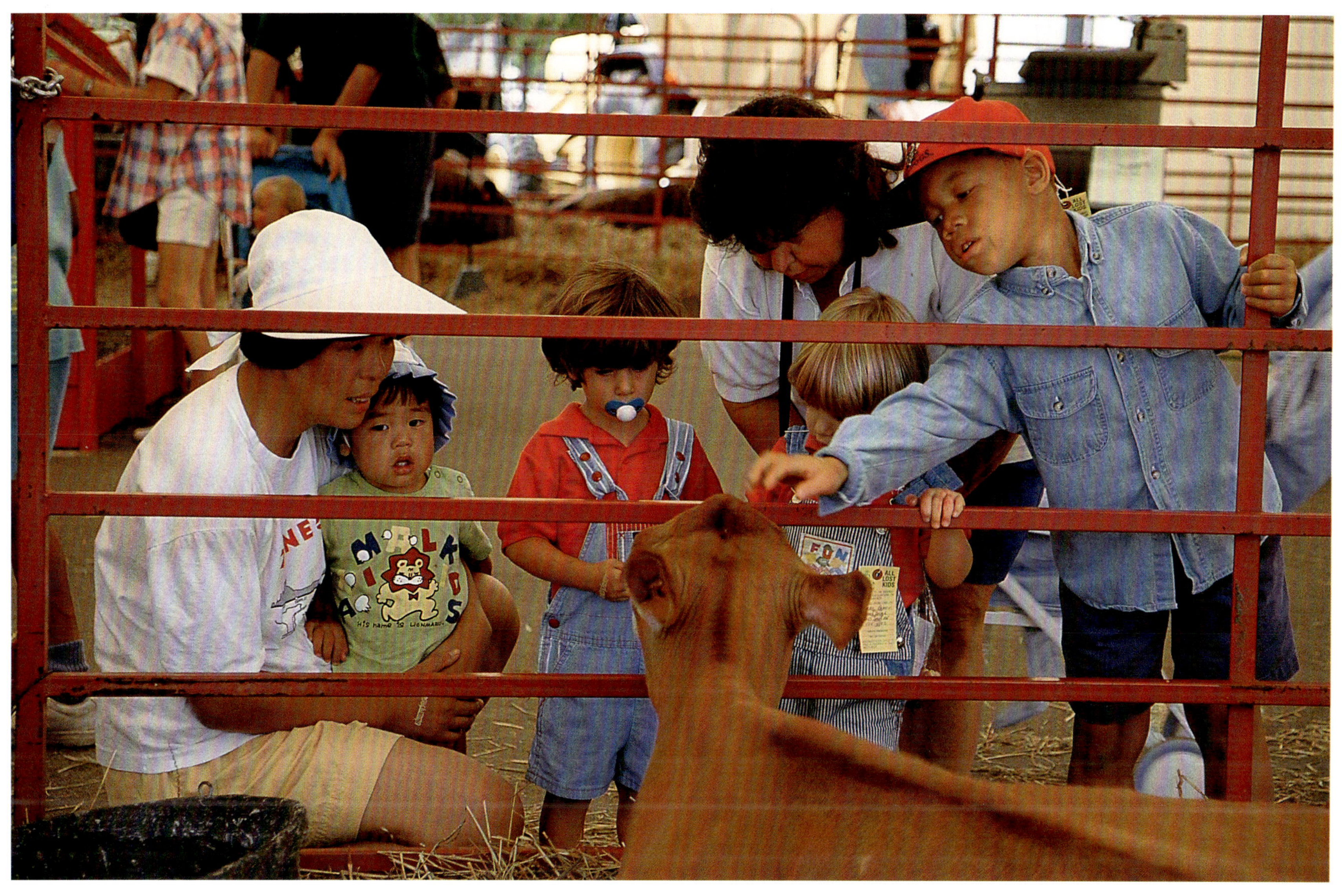

Drawing almost one million enthusiasts each year, the Ohio State Fair features thousands of animals and agricultural exhibits along with a midway and concert performances.

Columbus's German Village is named for the thousands of immigrants who flocked here in the mid-1800s, searching for freedom and prosperity. German schools, churches, and newspapers helped them retain some of their heritage.

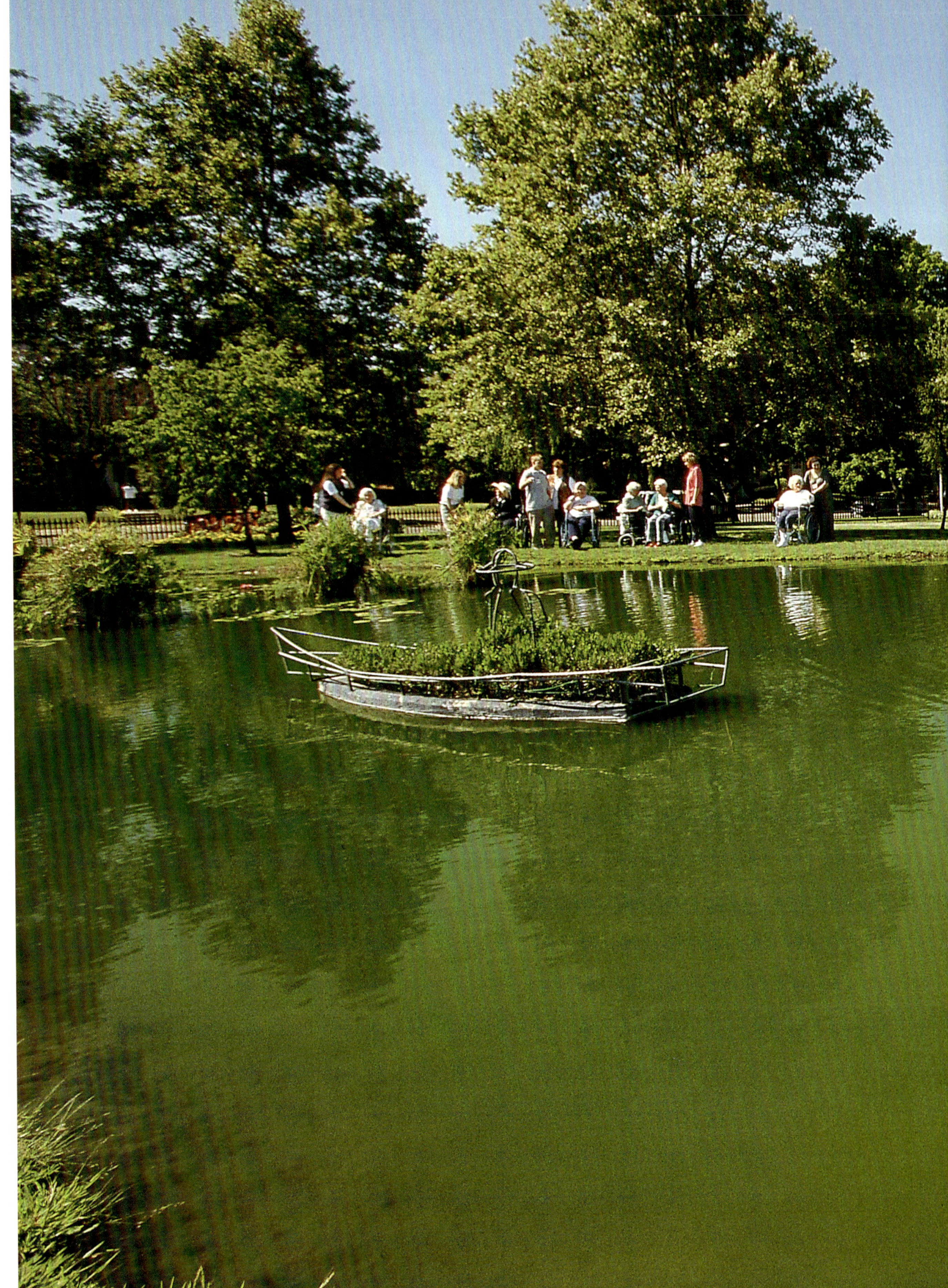

On the grounds of Columbus's Topiary Garden, landscapers have recreated Georges Seurat's famous painting *A Sunday on the Island of la Grande Jatte* completely in topiary. The installation includes people, boats, and animals arranged exactly as they are in the original painting.

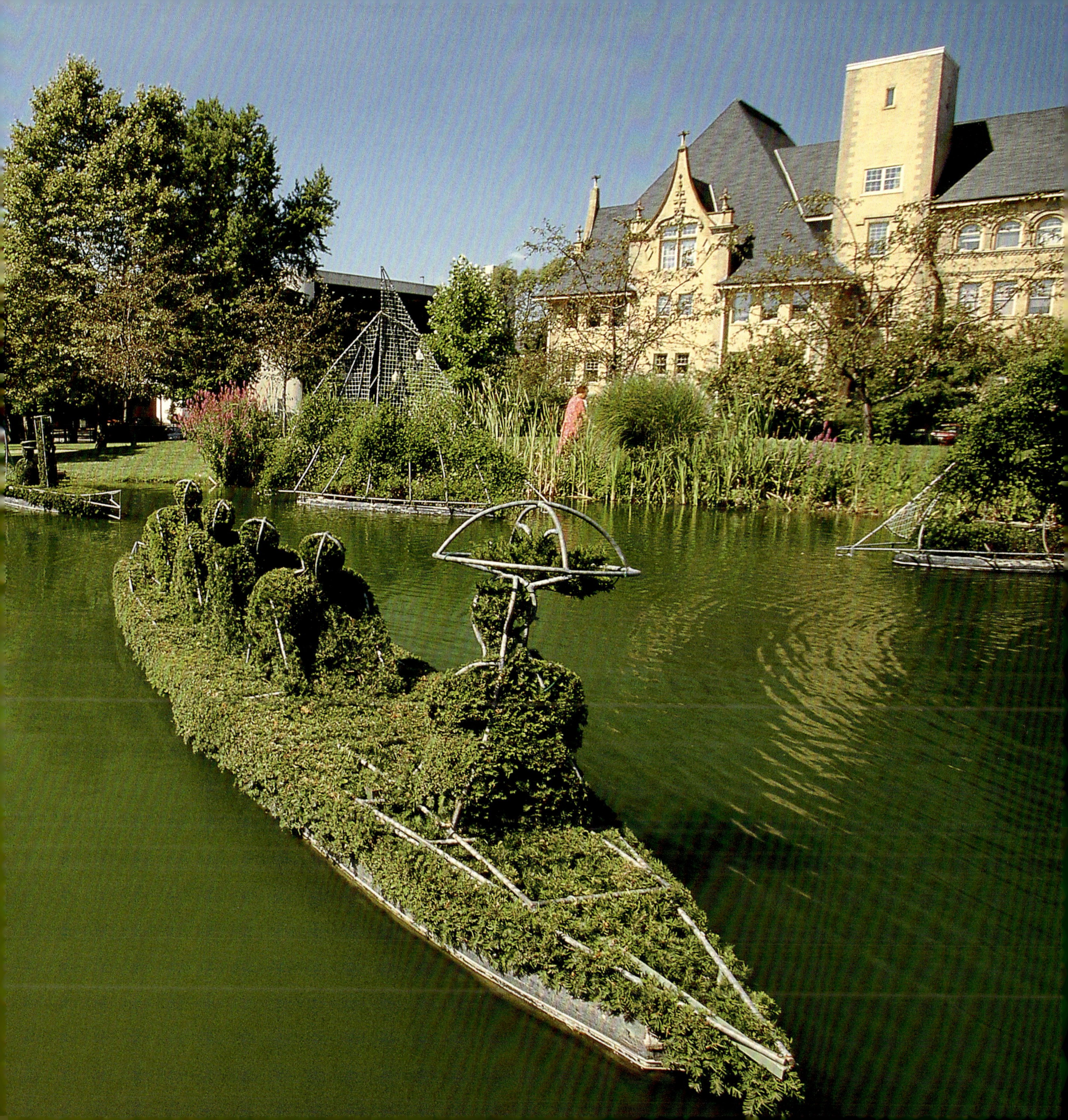

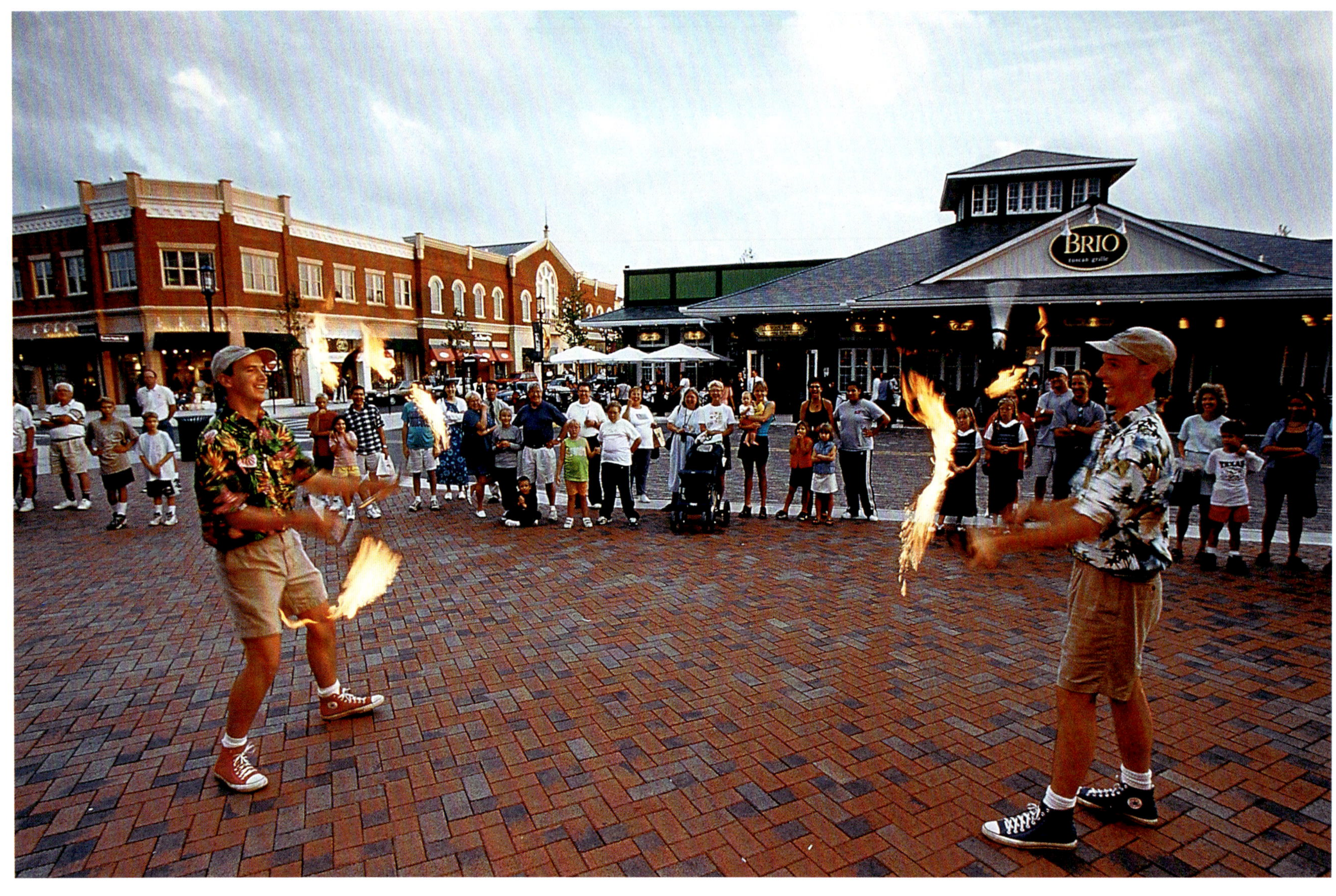

Fire jugglers draw a crowd outside of Easton Town Center in Columbus. Opened in 1999, the shopping district has a 30-screen theater complex and more stores than the renowned Mall of America in Minnesota.

Old Man's Cave State Park is named for Richard Rowe, who arrived in the valley in the late 1700s and explored much of the Hocking region. He lived as a hermit within the cave for much of his life and is buried under a ledge inside.

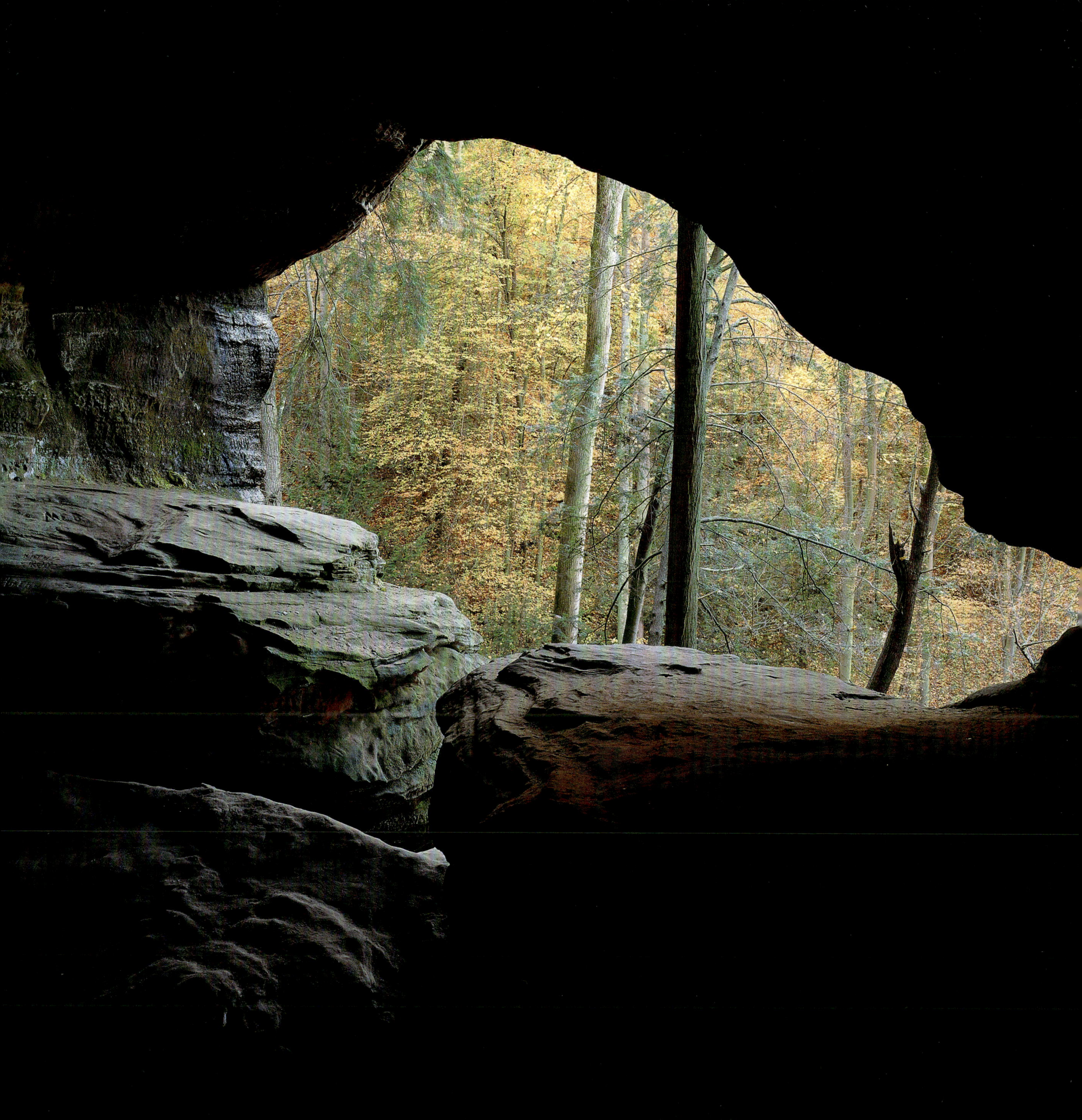

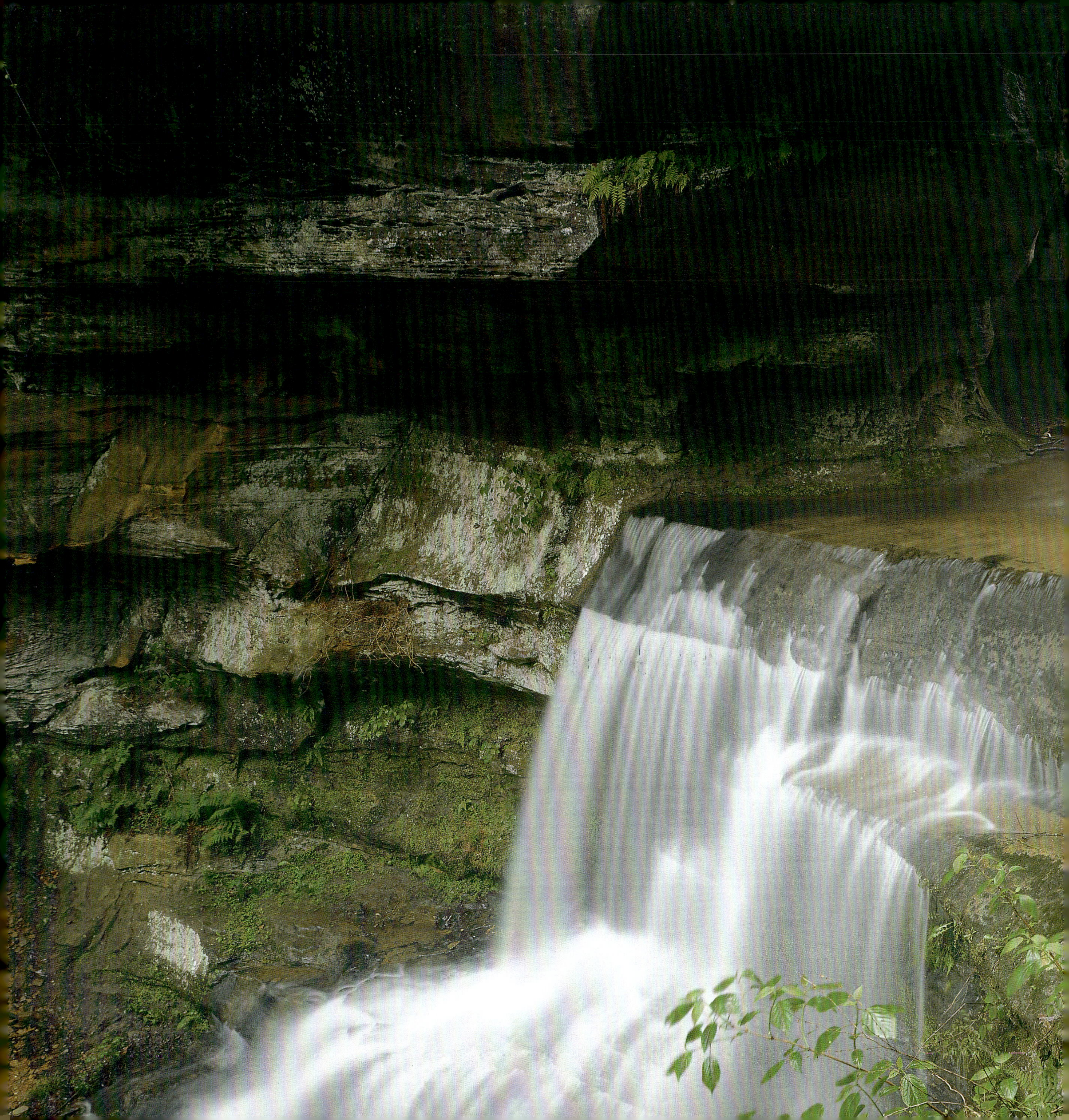

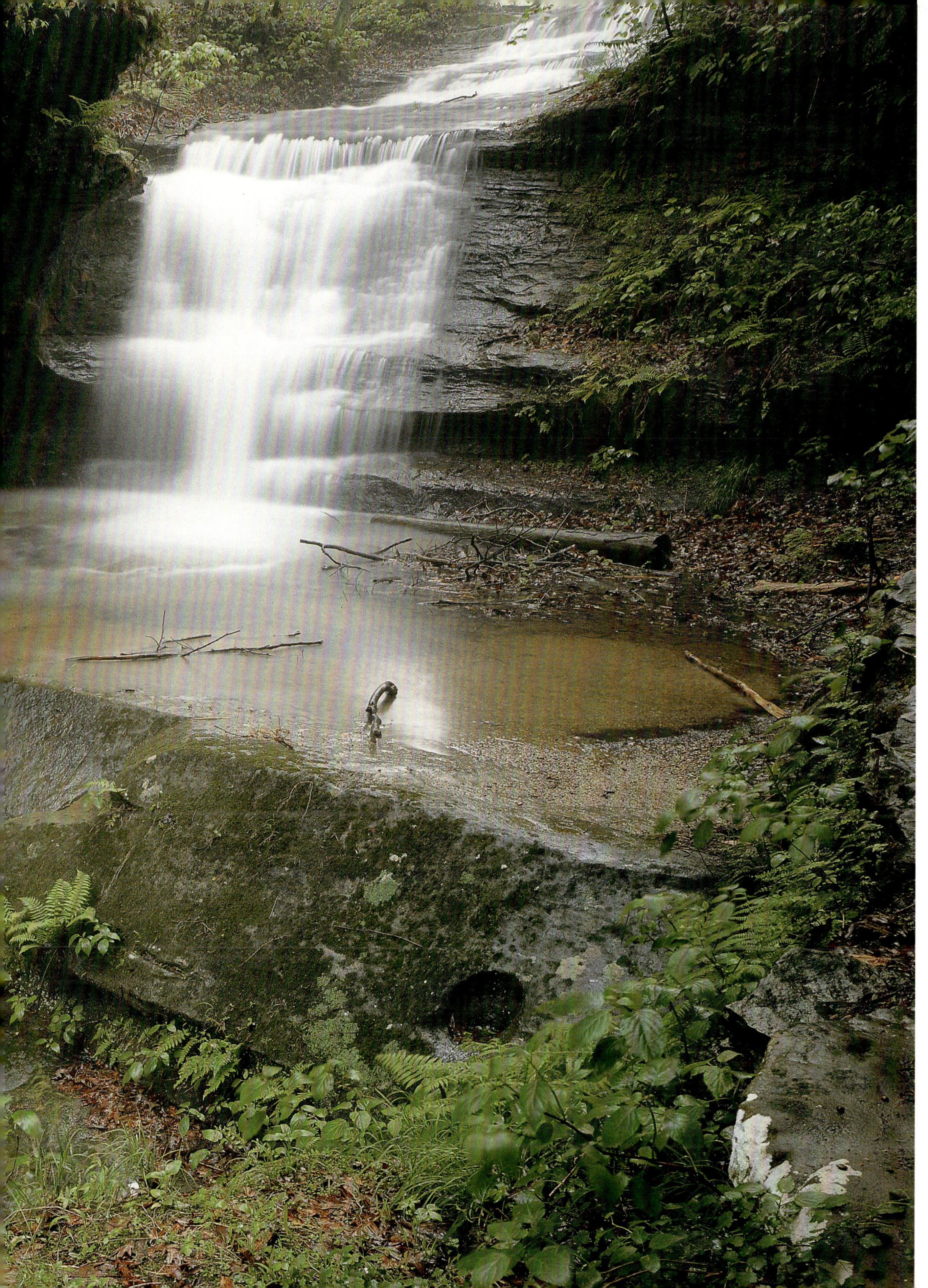

Old Man's Creek tumbles over four falls within Old Man's Cave State Park, before carving its way through the Lower Gorge. The banks of the creek reveal history, locked within Blackhand sandstone.

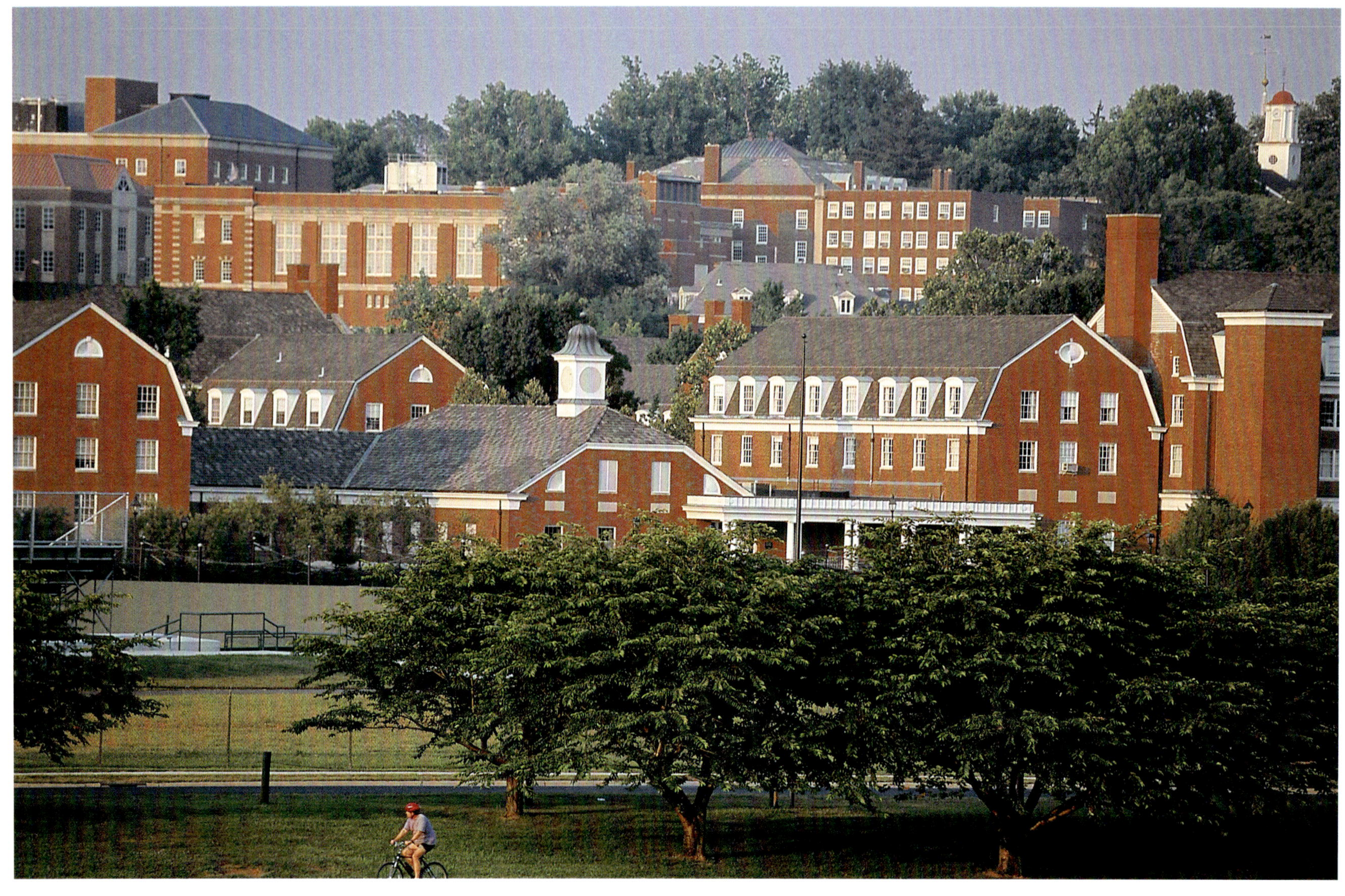

Ohio University in Athens has almost 20,000 students enrolled in a wide range of undergraduate and graduate programs. Students from 50 states and more than 100 countries attend classes here.

Hikers know the hills and canyons of Wayne National Forest as Ohio's Outback, where trails lead past hardwood groves, native pine stands, rare fern species, and mountain laurels.

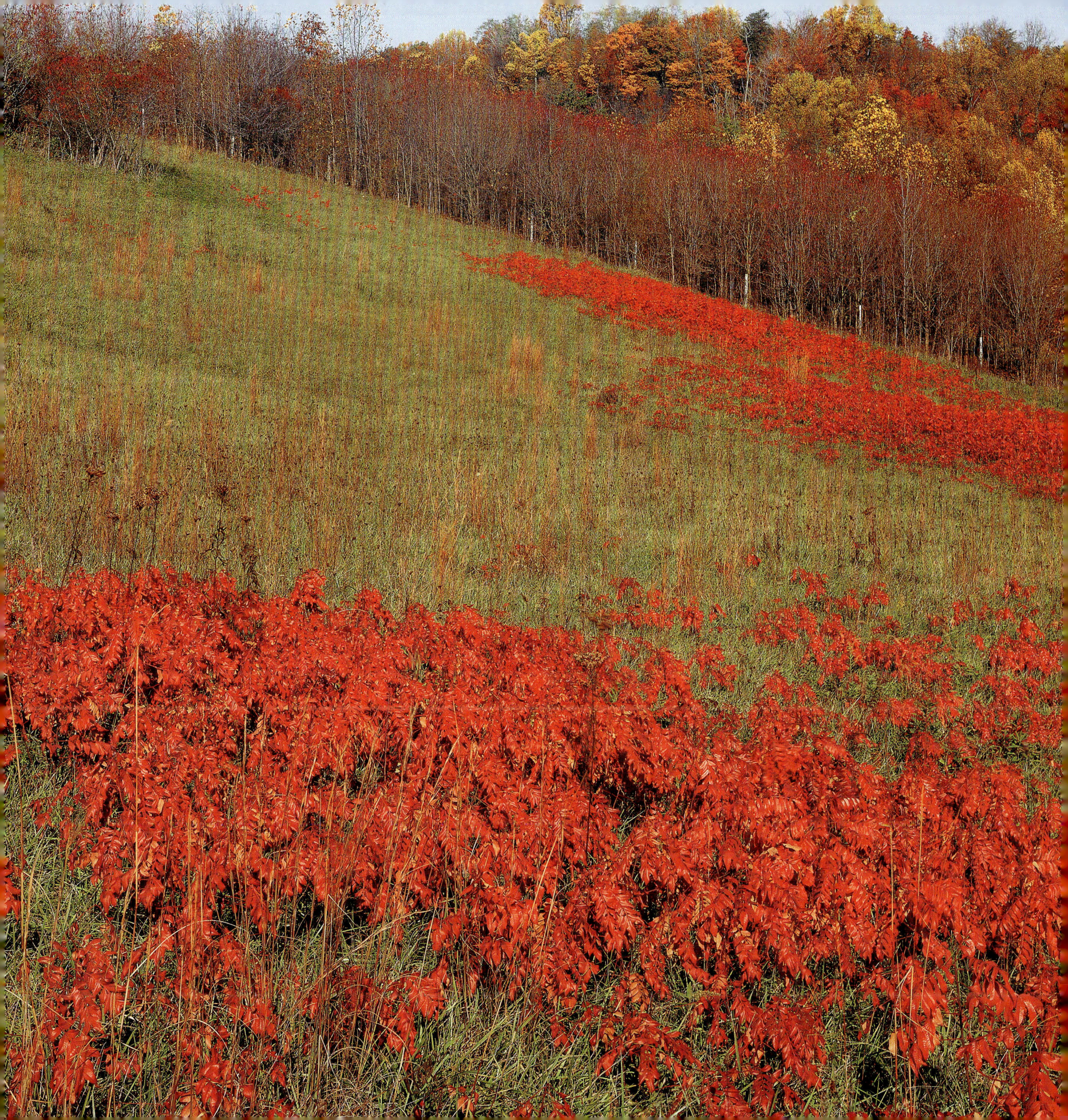

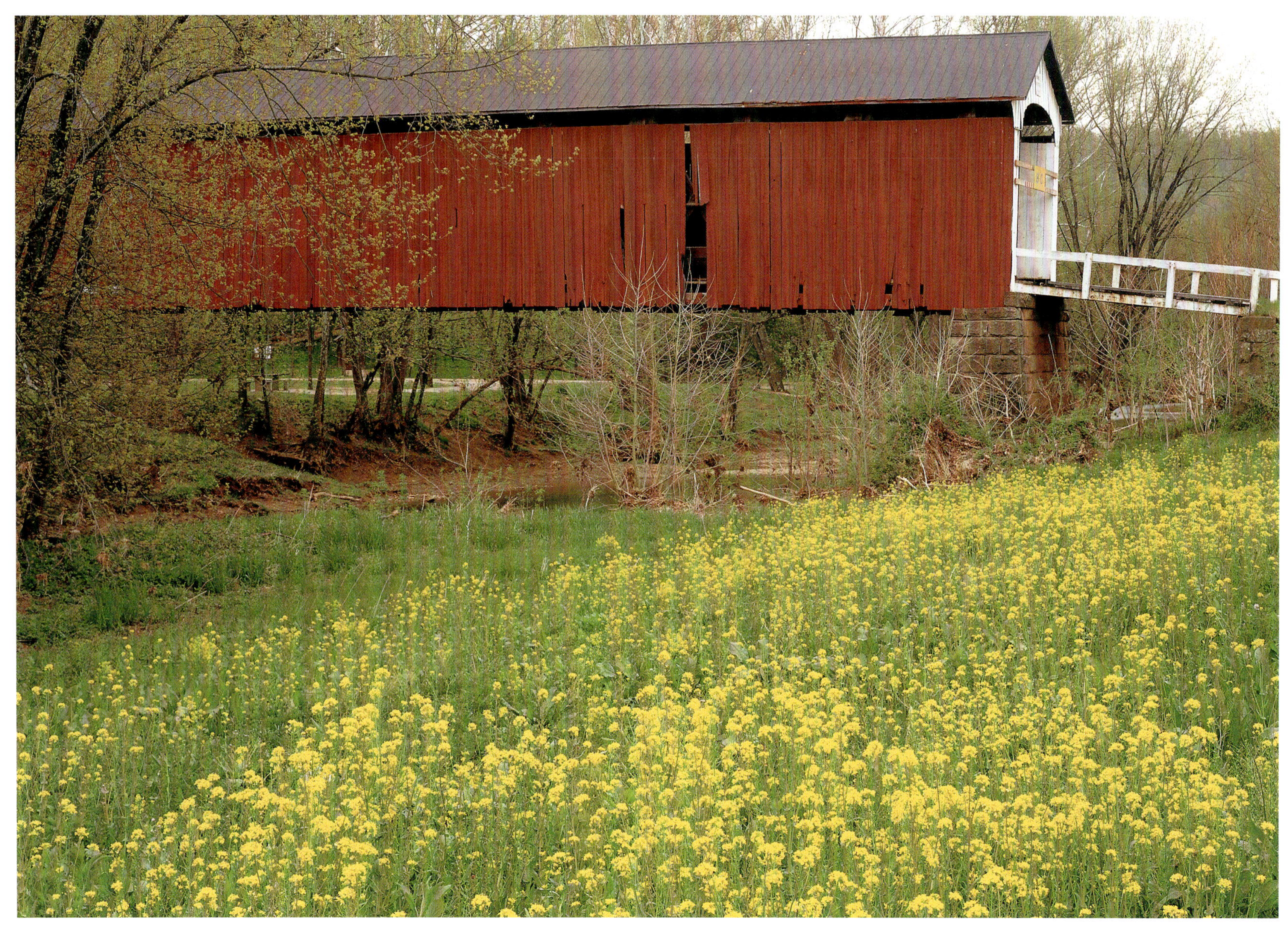

When the Depression forced many of southeastern Ohio's settlers from their homes, the farms of the region fell quickly into disrepair. The federal government eventually purchased 210,000 acres to form Wayne National Forest, where reminders of the area's early history can still be seen.

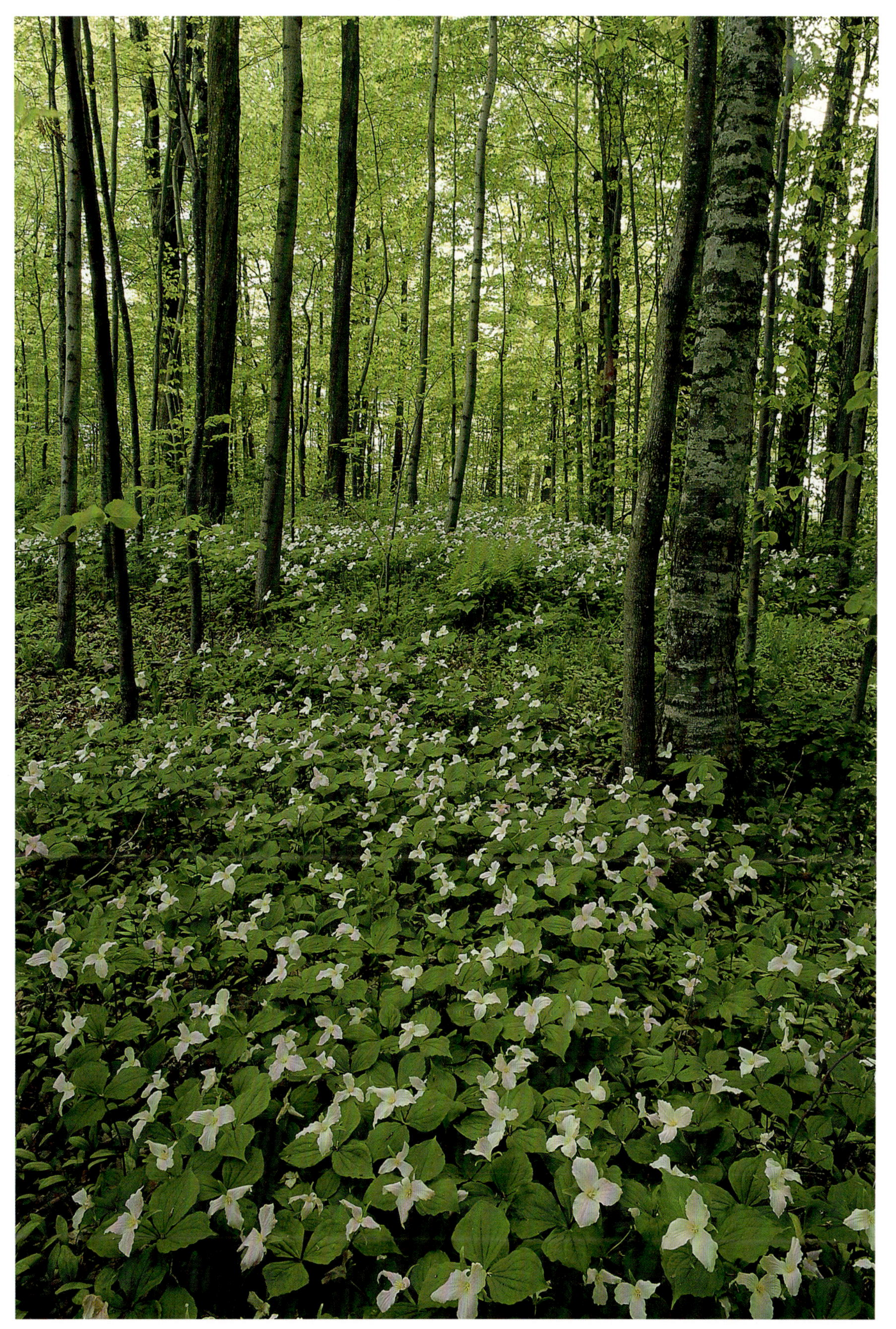

Announcing spring in the damp undergrowth of Wayne National Forest, these large-flowered trilliums bloom only a few inches above the ground, the flowers supported by the plant's broad leaves.

Winding 981 miles from Pittsburgh, Pennsylvania, to Cairo, Illinois, the Ohio River is a pristine haven for boaters and anglers. Some historians believe *Ohio* comes from an Iroquois word meaning beautiful.

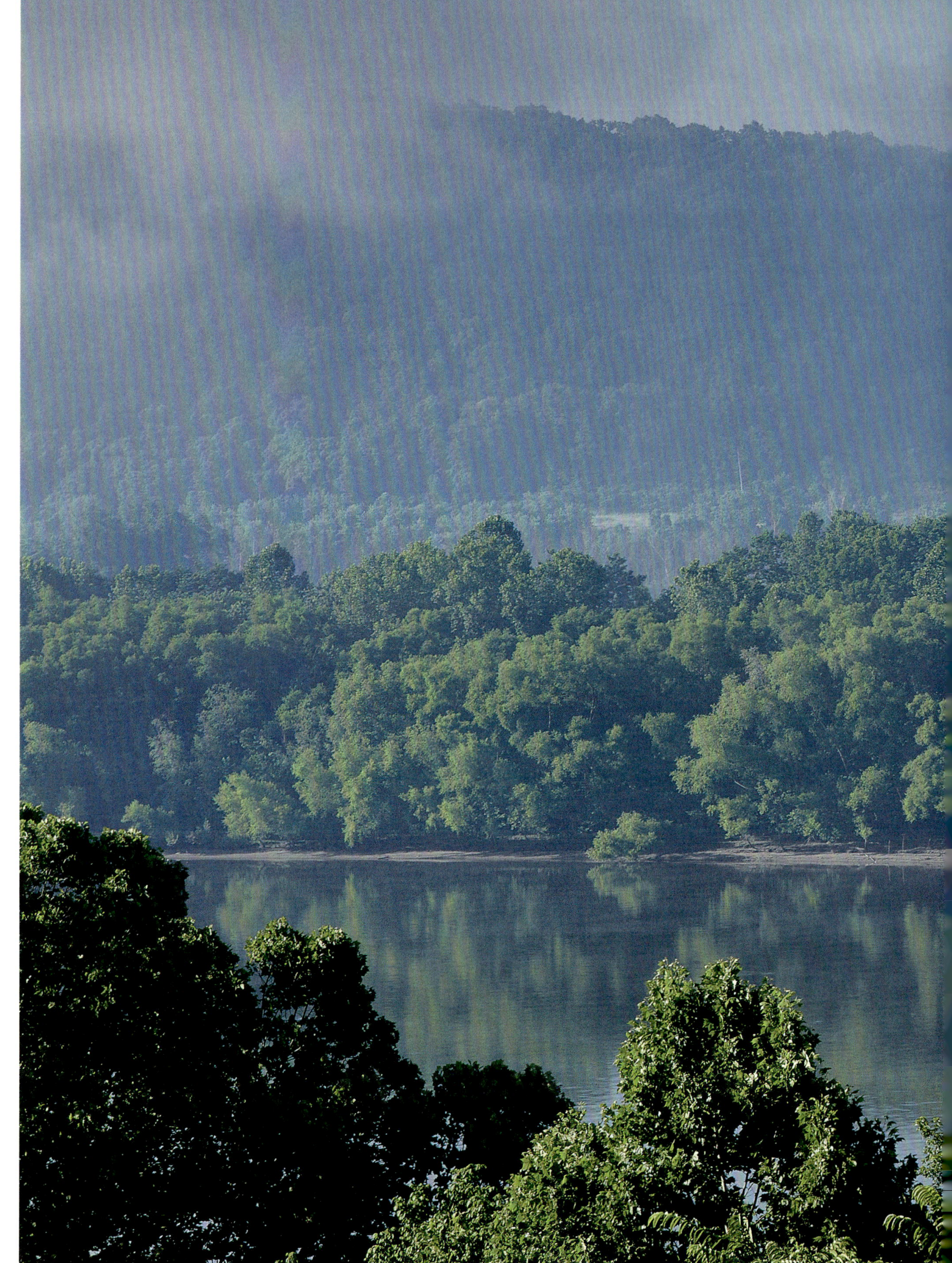

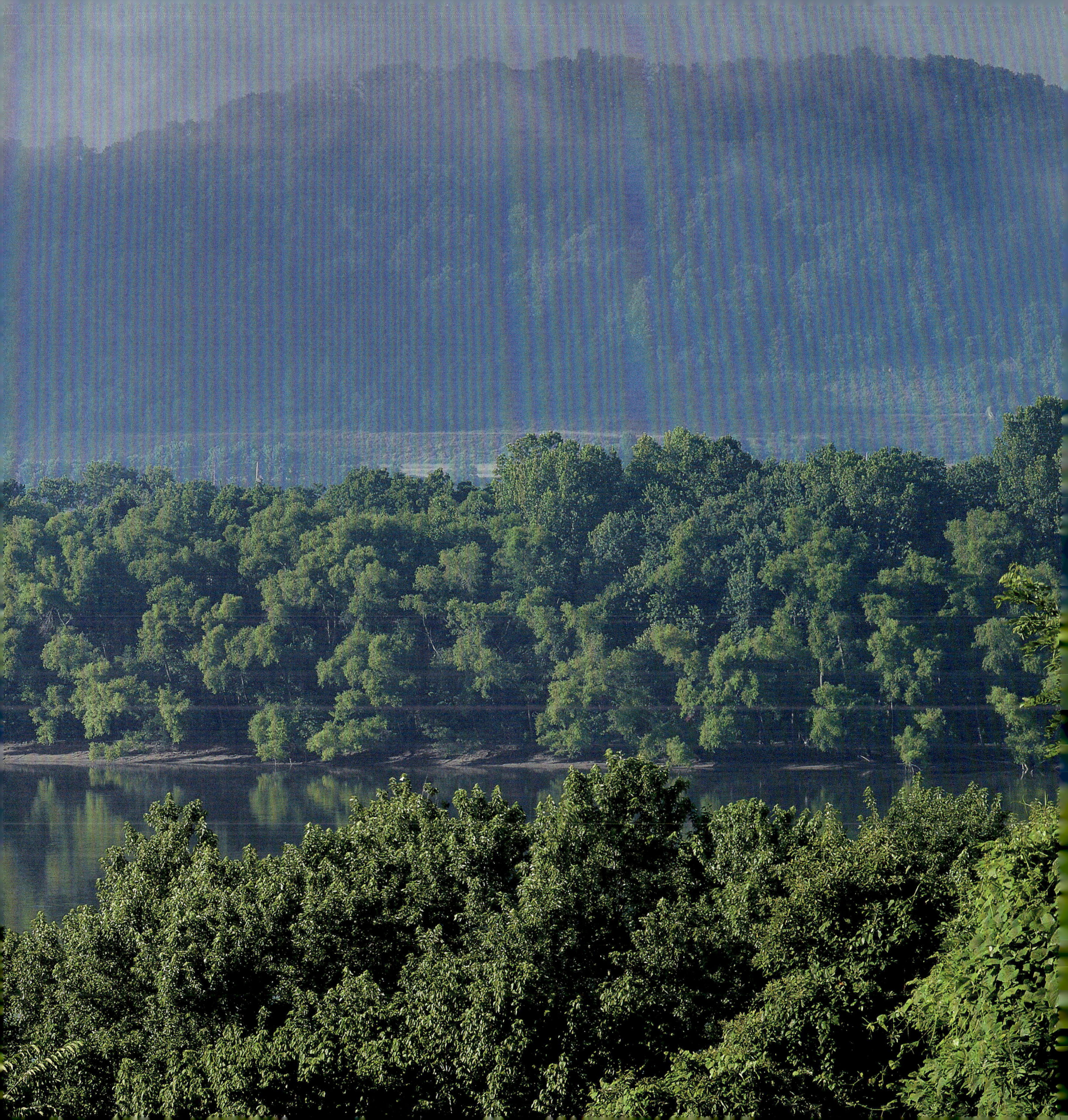

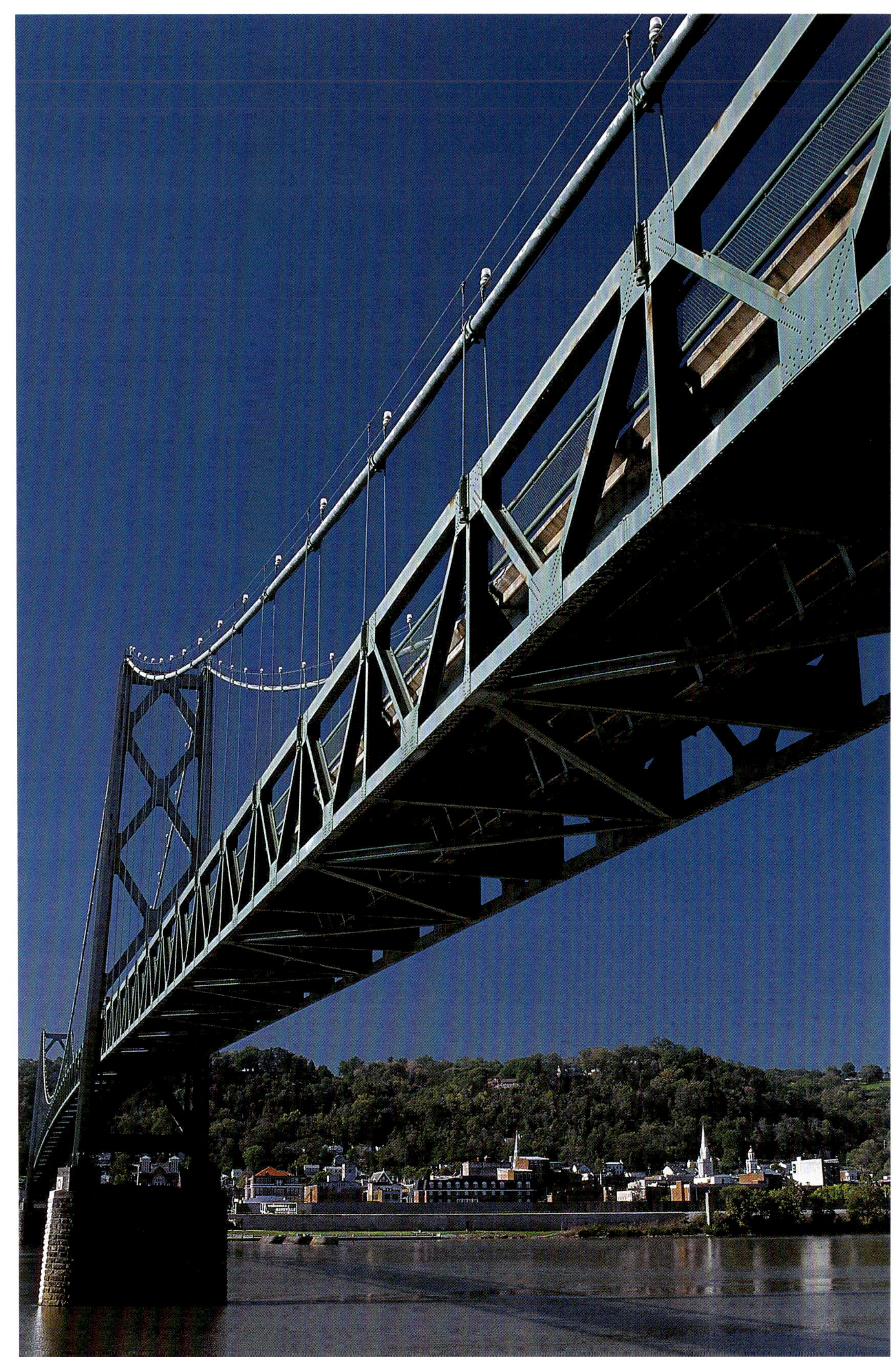

The concrete span across the Ohio River at Aberdeen is 2,100 feet long and specially designed to remain stable even in high winds. The bridge's engineers won several major awards for their achievement.

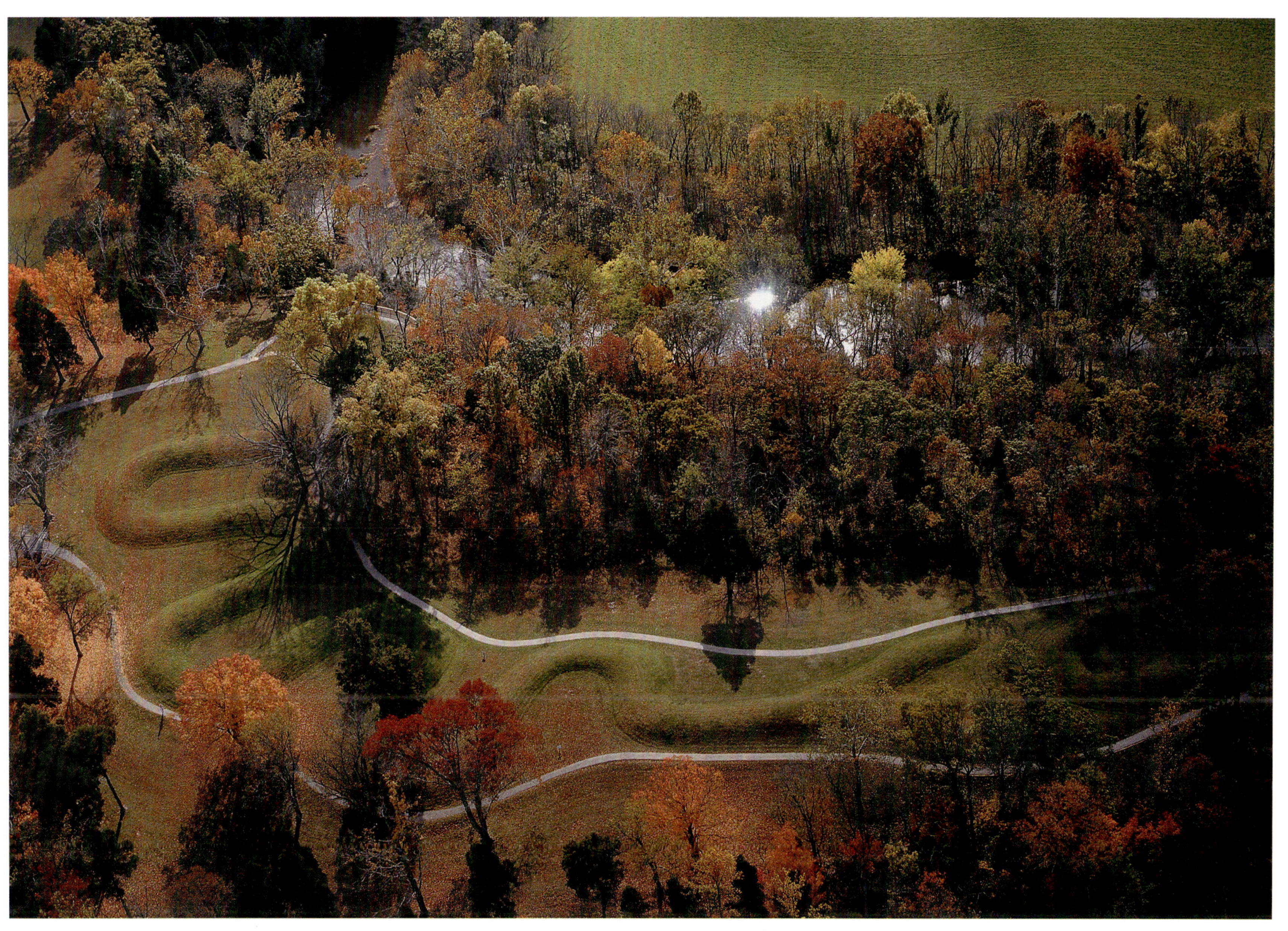

No one knows exactly how or why the Serpent Mound was created, but archaeologists believe the quarter-mile-long coils had religious significance to the Adena people who lived here more than 2,000 years ago.

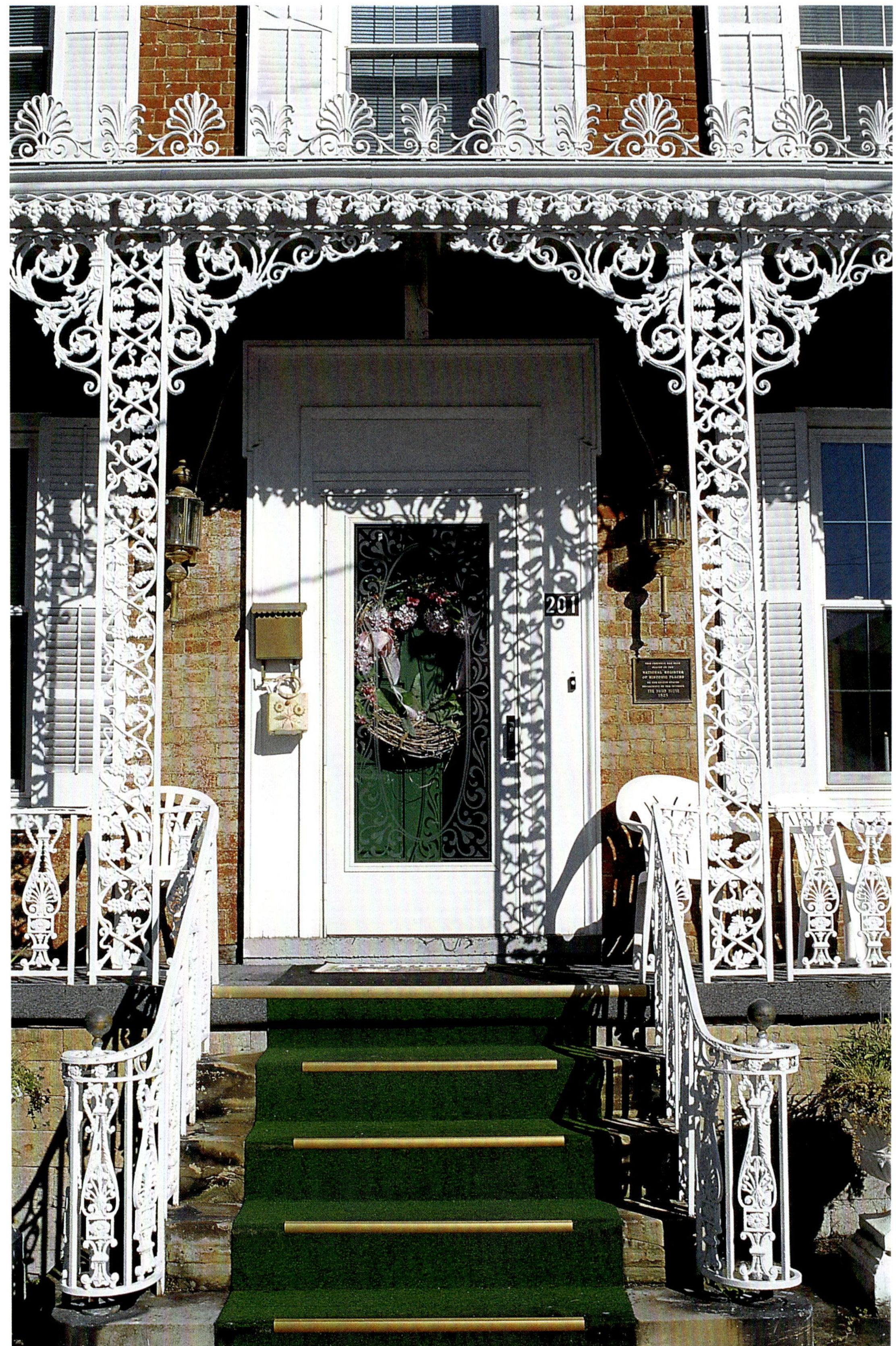

The picturesque village of Ripley is best known for its role in the abolitionist movement of the early nineteenth century. The story immortalized in *Uncle Tom's Cabin* is based on the true tale of a slave who escaped across the Ohio River to find safety here.

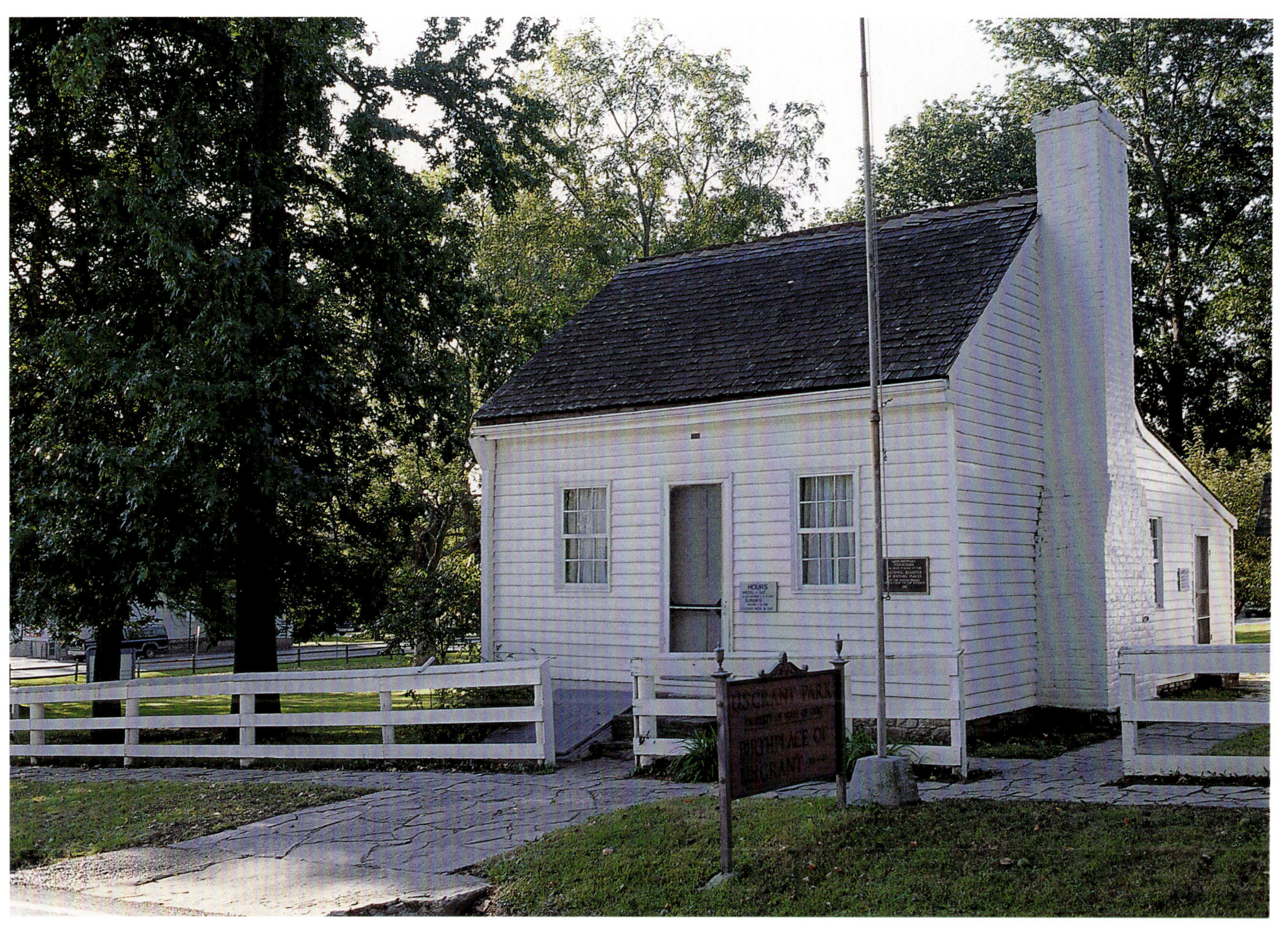

President Ulysses S. Grant spent his childhood in and around this quaint home in Point Pleasant. After fighting in the Civil War, Grant served from 1869 to 1877 as the eighteenth president of the United States. He died in 1885.

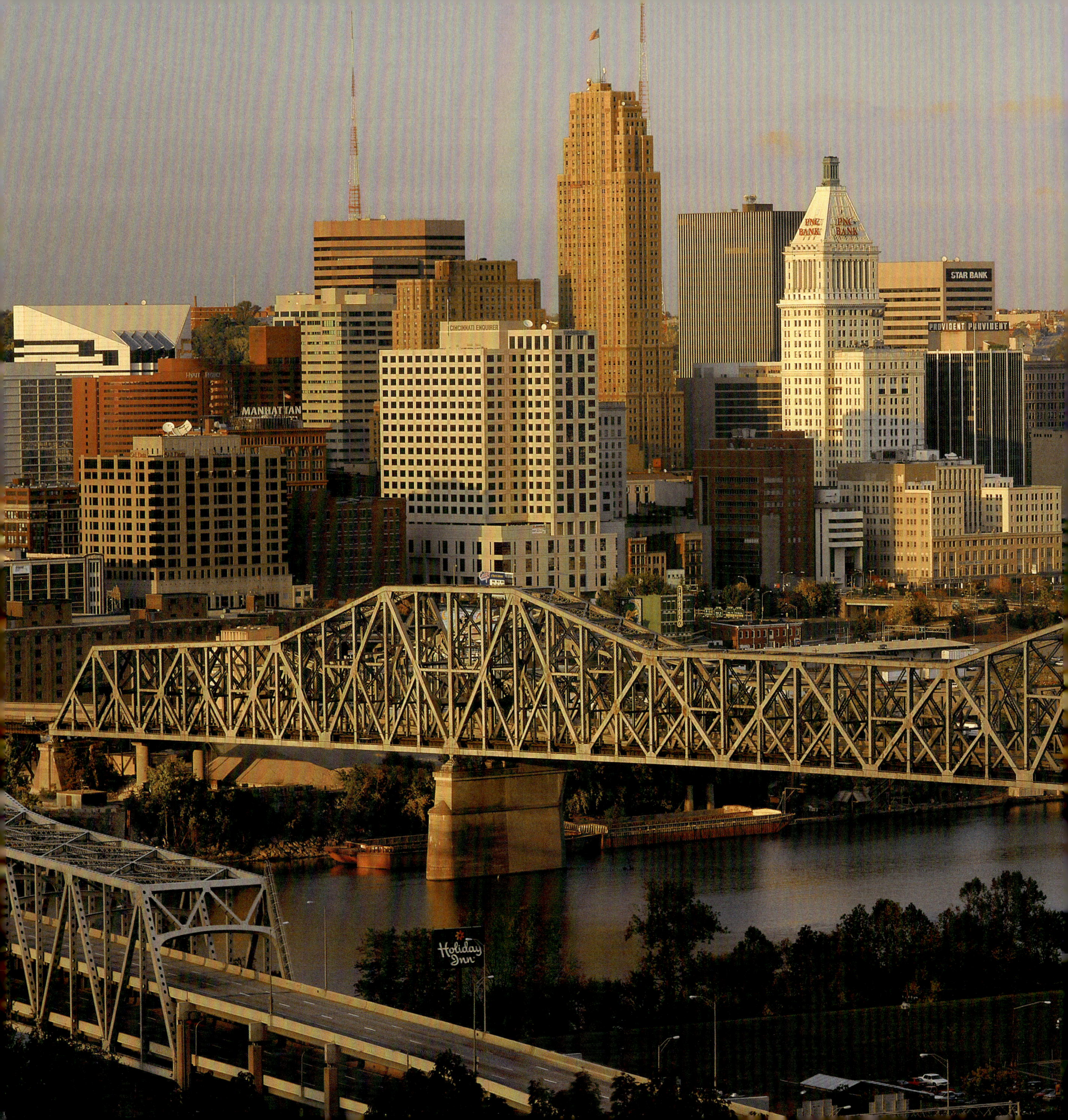
PNC BANK
STAR BANK
CINCINNATI ENQUIRER
MANHATTAN
Holiday Inn

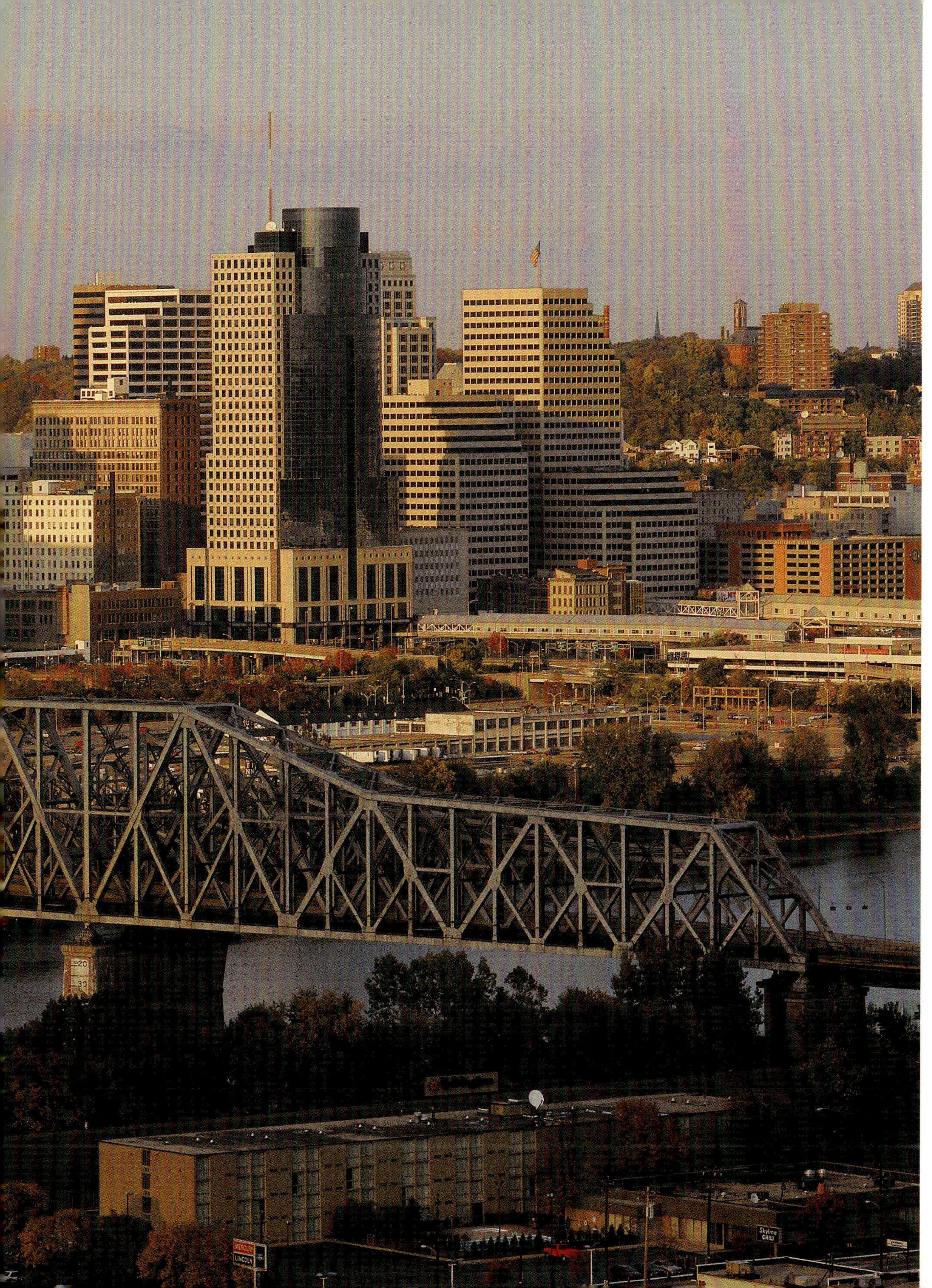

Cincinnati revelers are known for their love of two things — baseball and beer. The first began when the Cincinnati Reds began playing here in the late 1800s. The beer had already been flowing for nearly a century by then, thanks to an influx of German brewmasters.

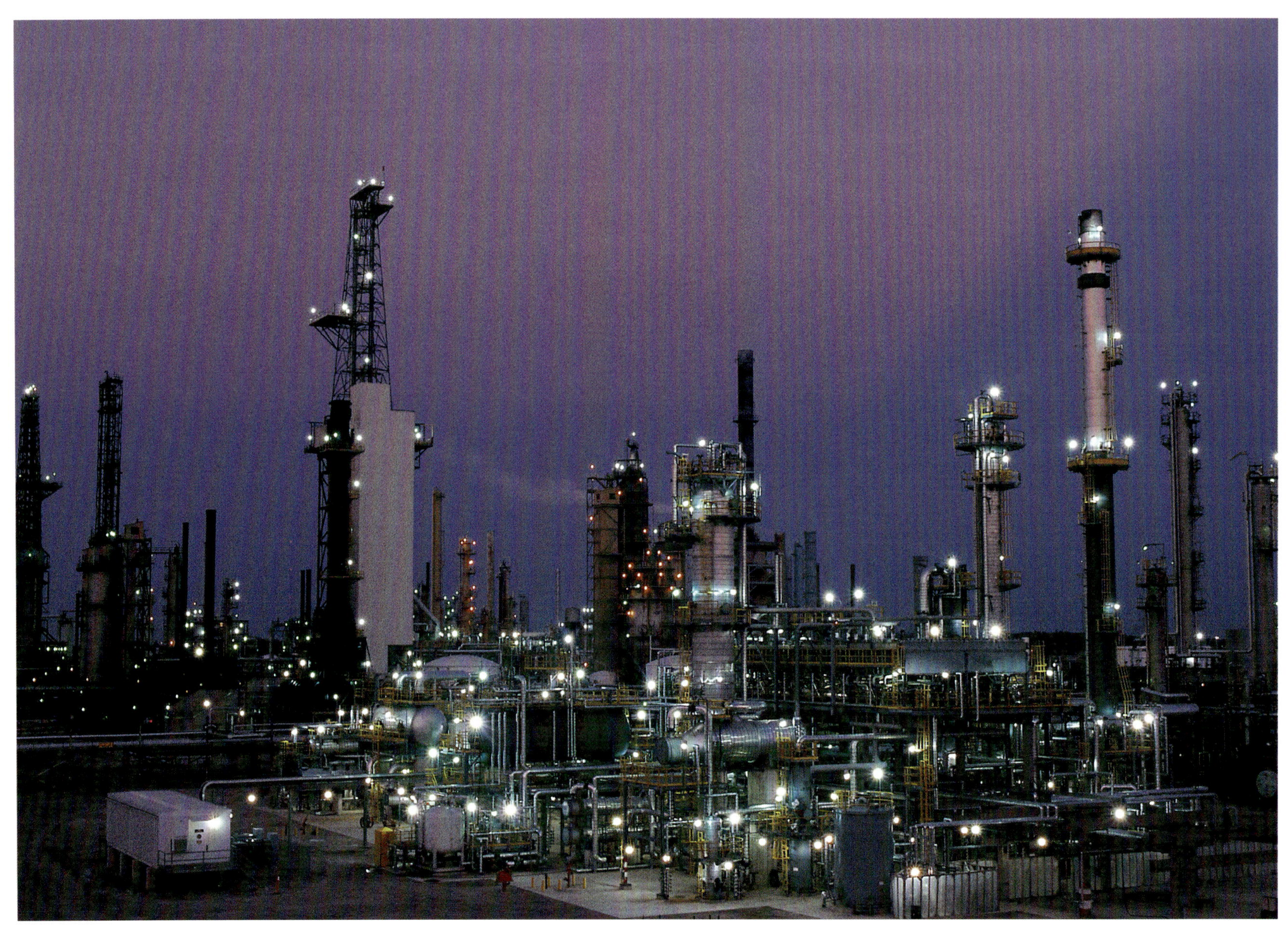

There are more than 63,000 active oil wells in Ohio, most plumbing the rich oil fields of the east. The state's refineries produce enough oil and gas to heat a million homes each year.

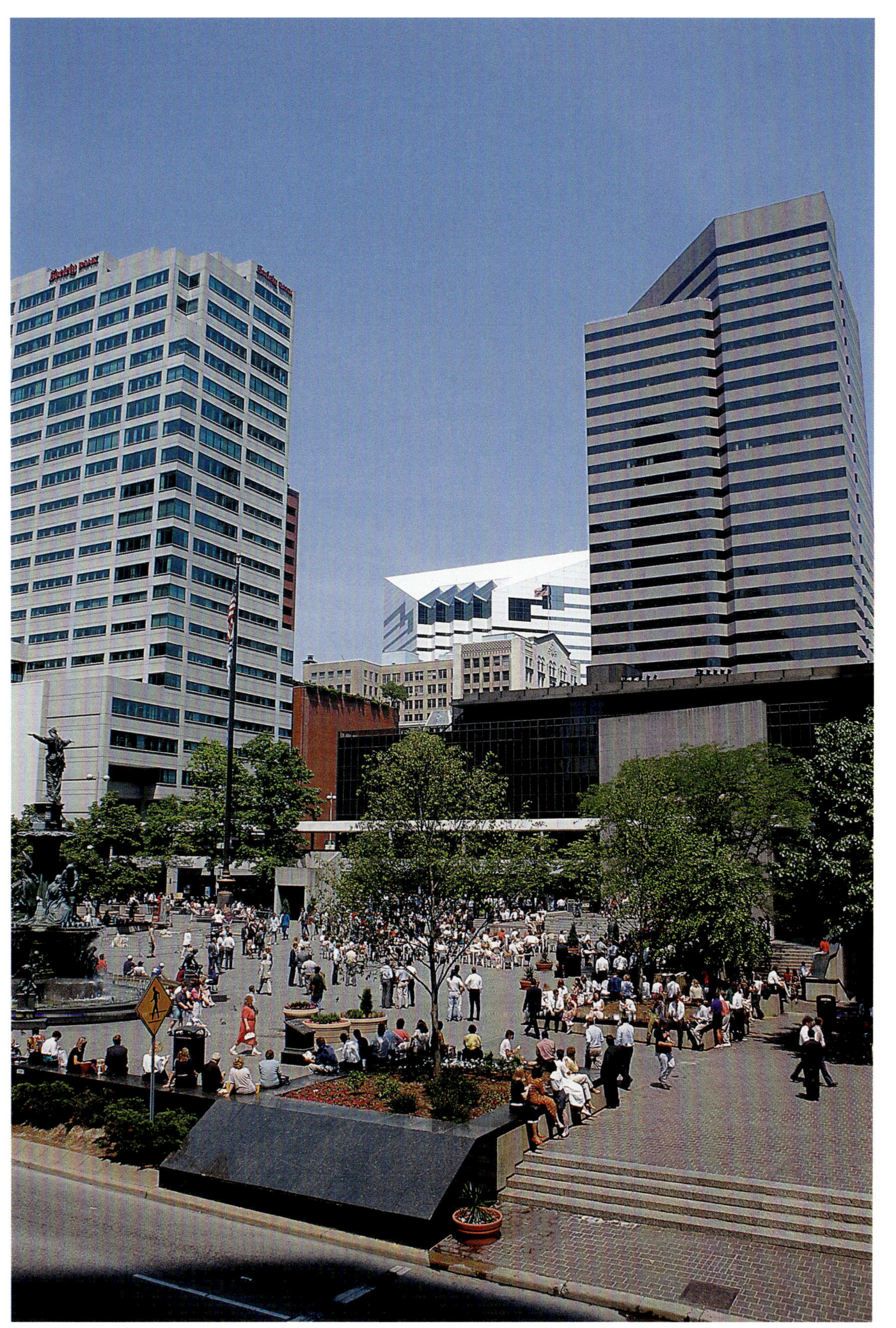

Cincinnati was named after the Society of Cincinnatus, an association founded by George Washington for officers of the Revolutionary War. The city has also been dubbed Porkopolis, for its history of meat packing.

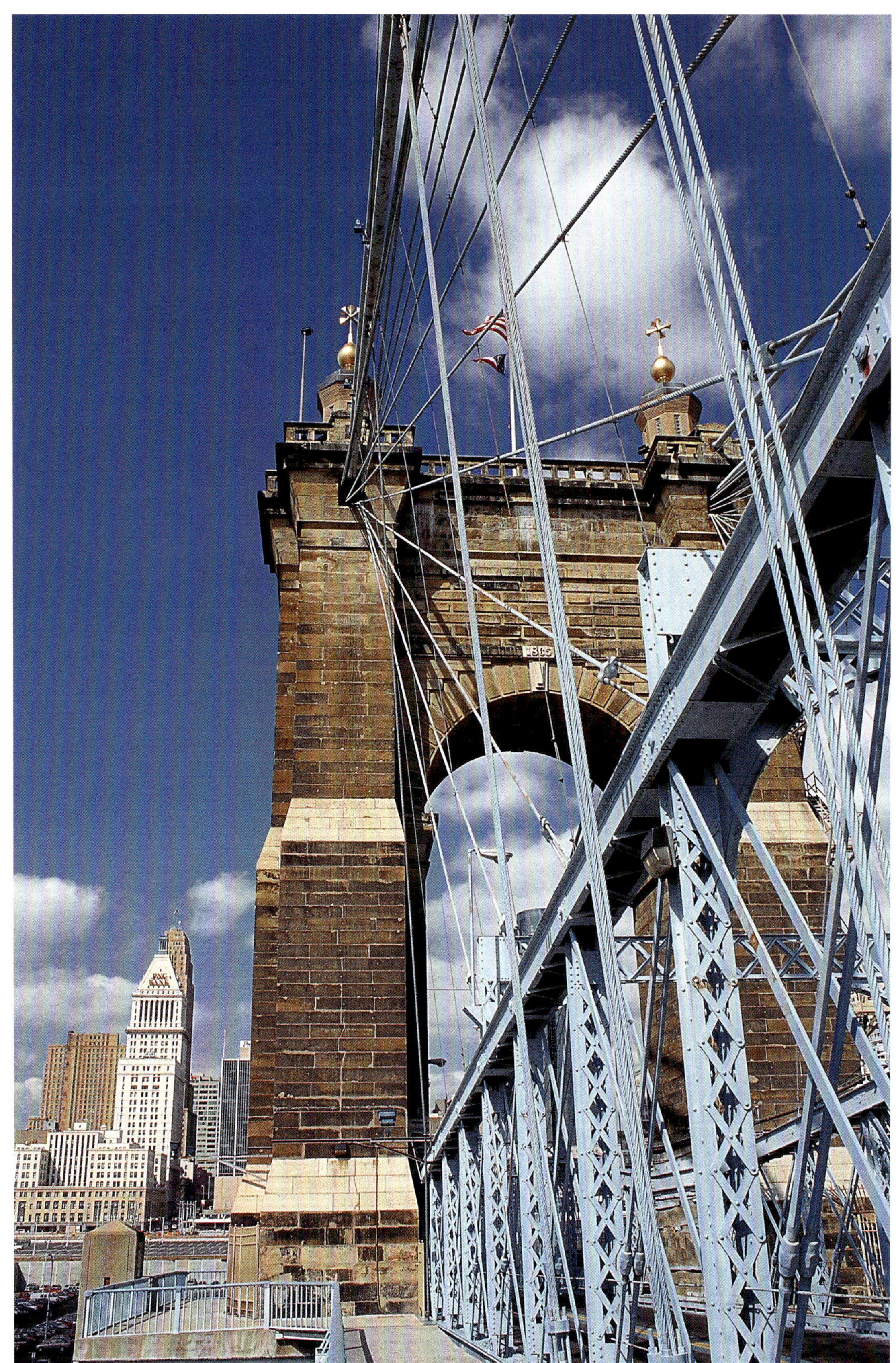

Linking Cincinnati with Covington, Kentucky, this bridge was designed by renowned engineer John A. Roebling. His crews began construction in the fall of 1856 and finished the 2,252-foot span the following spring.

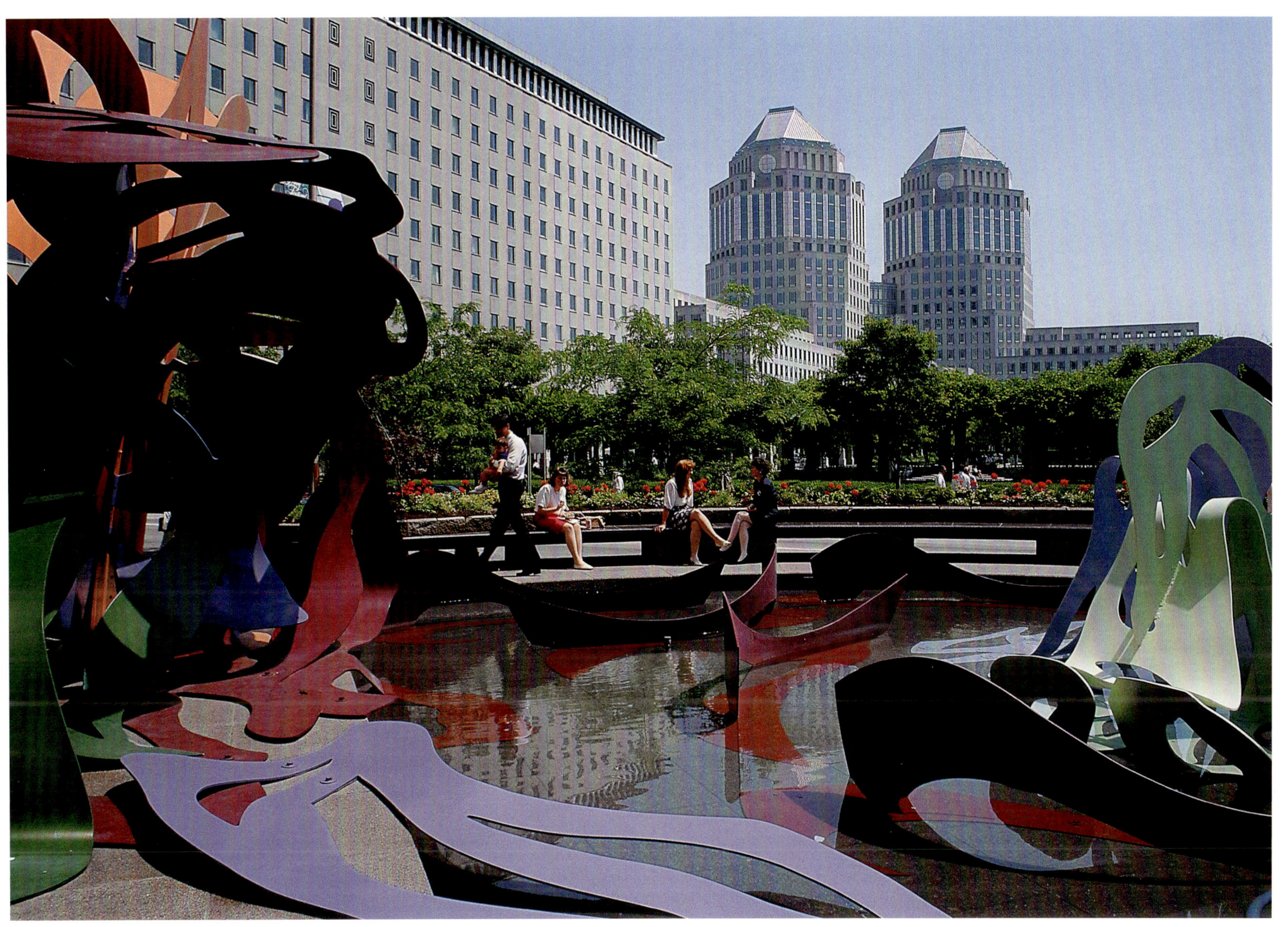

George Sugarman's sculpture *Cincinnati Story,* a colorful aluminum structure with moving water below, reflects the constant activity of Chiquita Plaza.

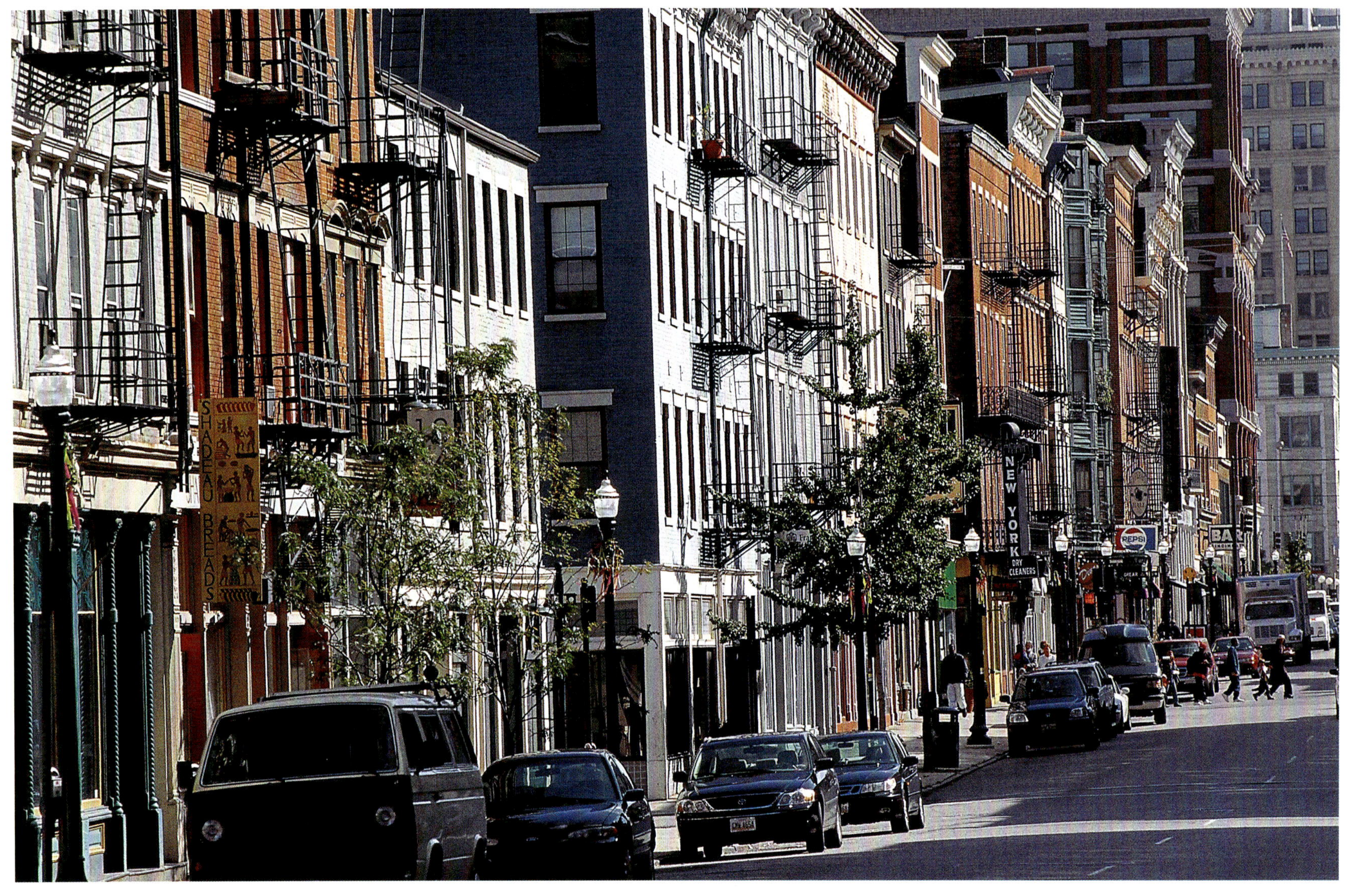

Residents and tourists seeking evening entertainment will likely find themselves on Cincinnati's Main Street, where upscale eateries and trendy nightclubs offer something for everyone.

The first park in Hamilton County, Sharon Woods was set aside in 1932; today it is home to deer, small mammals, and many bird species. Schoolchildren explore displays in the park's visitor center, while naturalists lead walks through the evergreens.

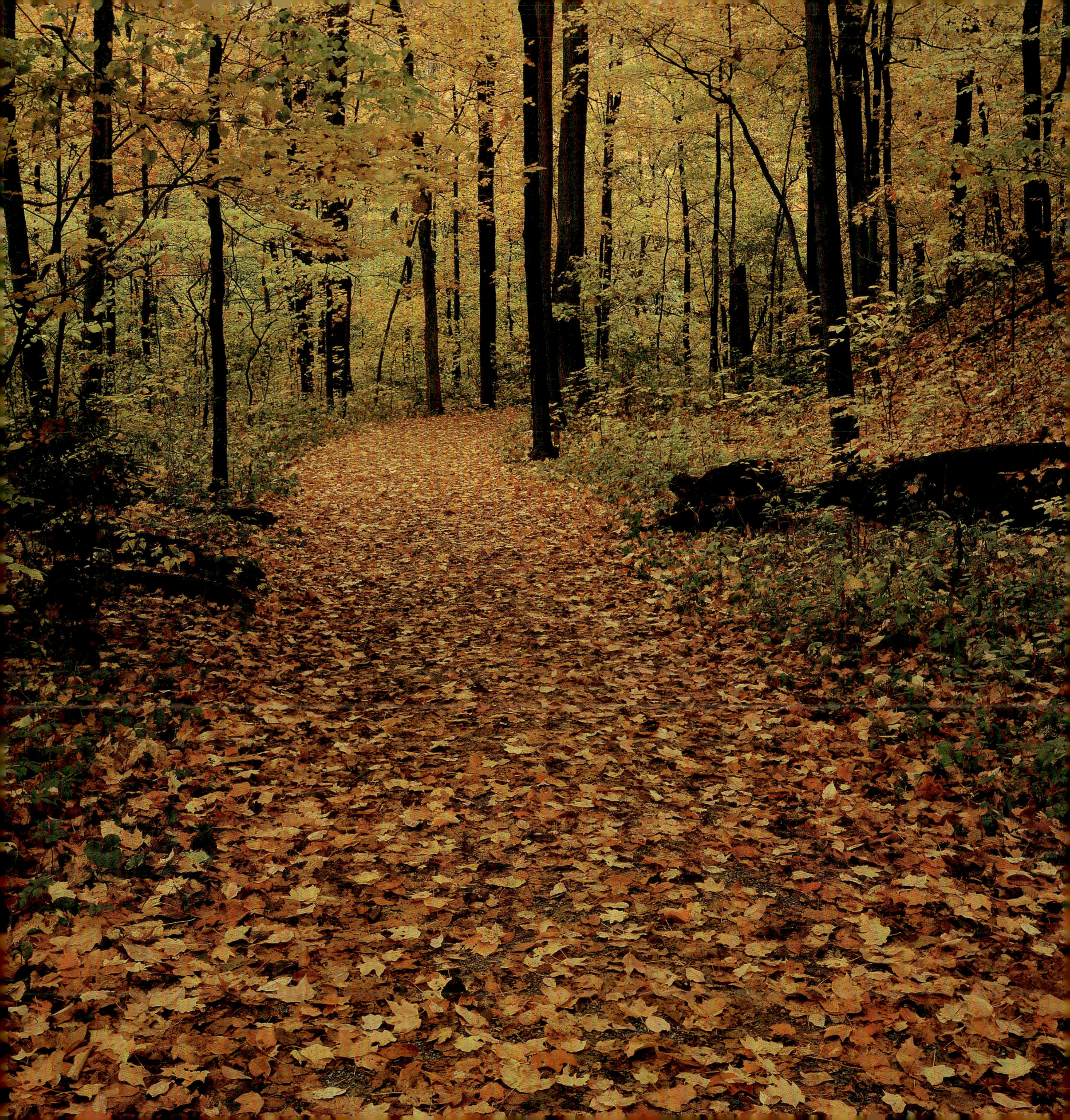

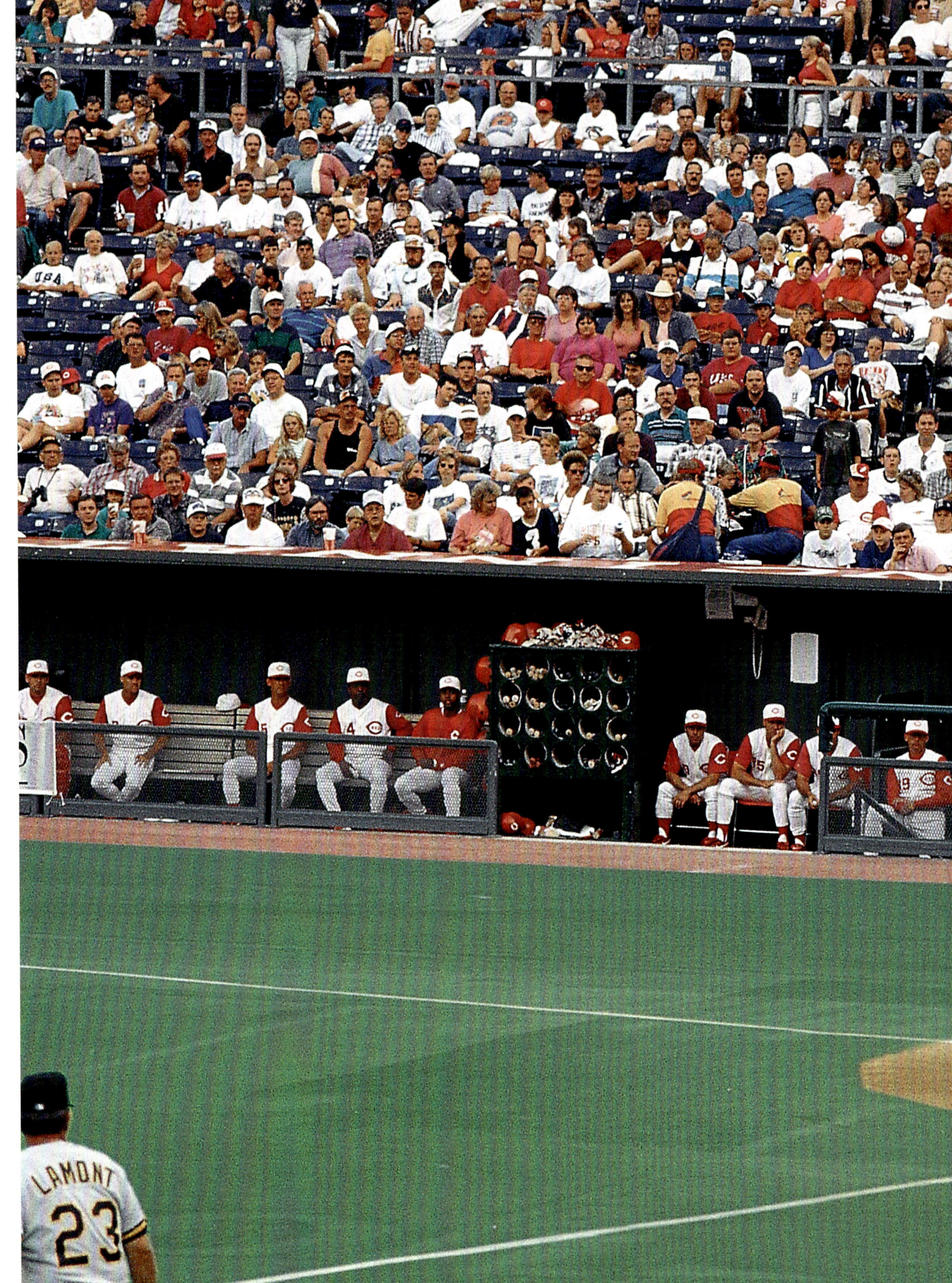

The Cincinnati Reds were the nation's first professional baseball team. They won their game against the Mansfield Independents in 1869, 48 to 14. More than a century later, fans fill Riverfront Stadium to the rafters.

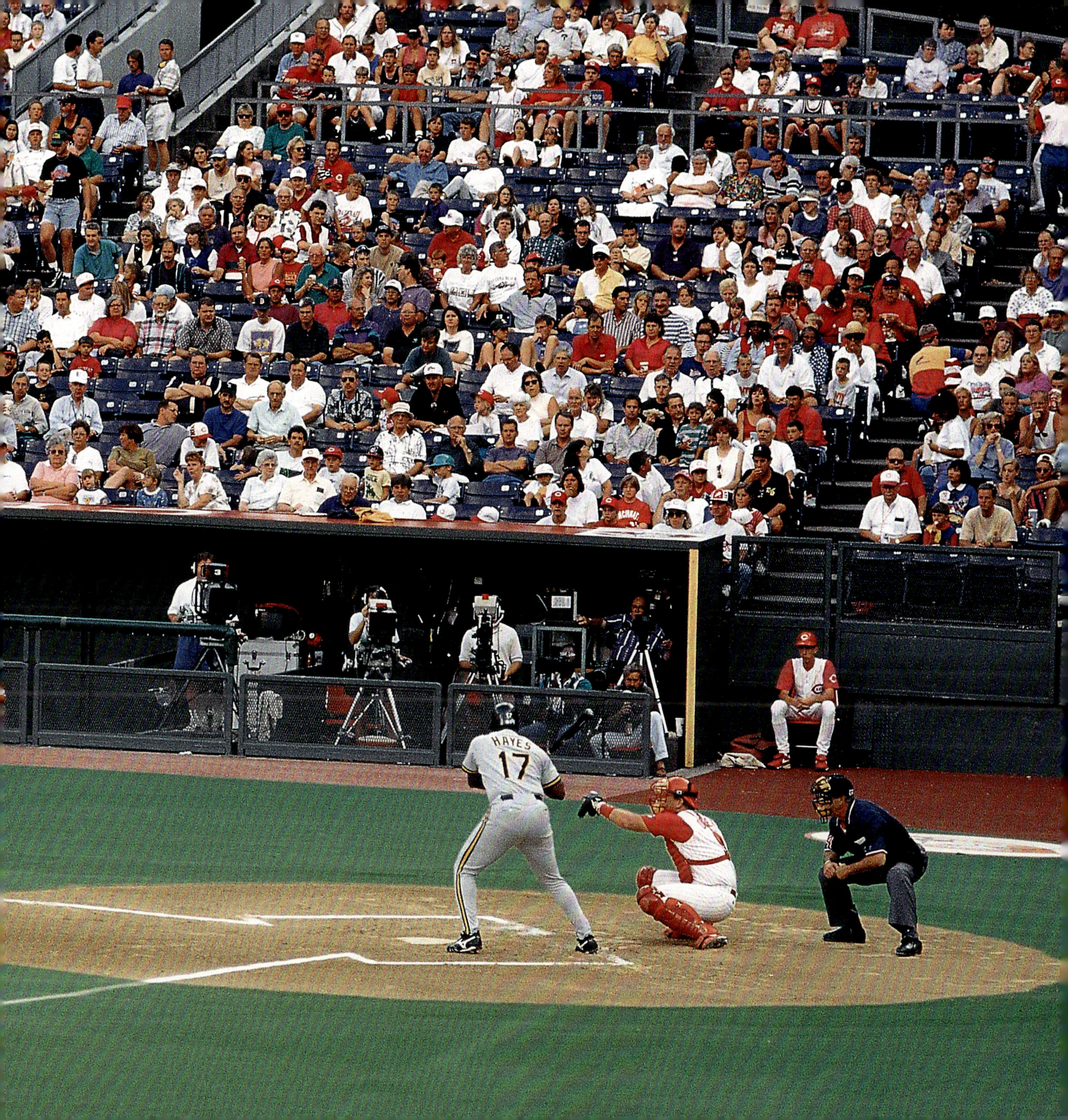
HAYES
17

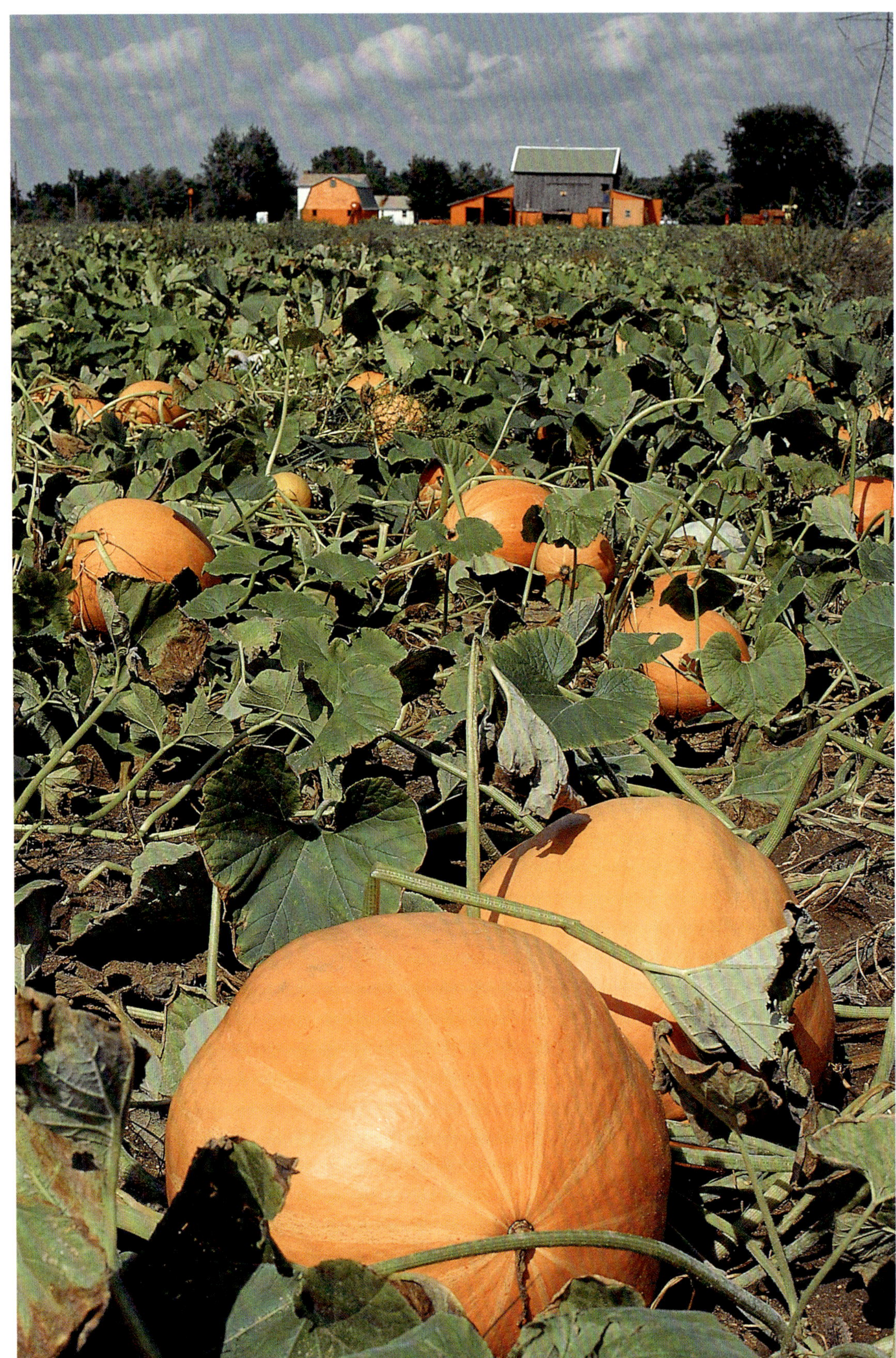

There are about 73,000 farms in the state, totaling 15 million acres. Ohio is one of the only states in America where more than half the land is ideal for farming.

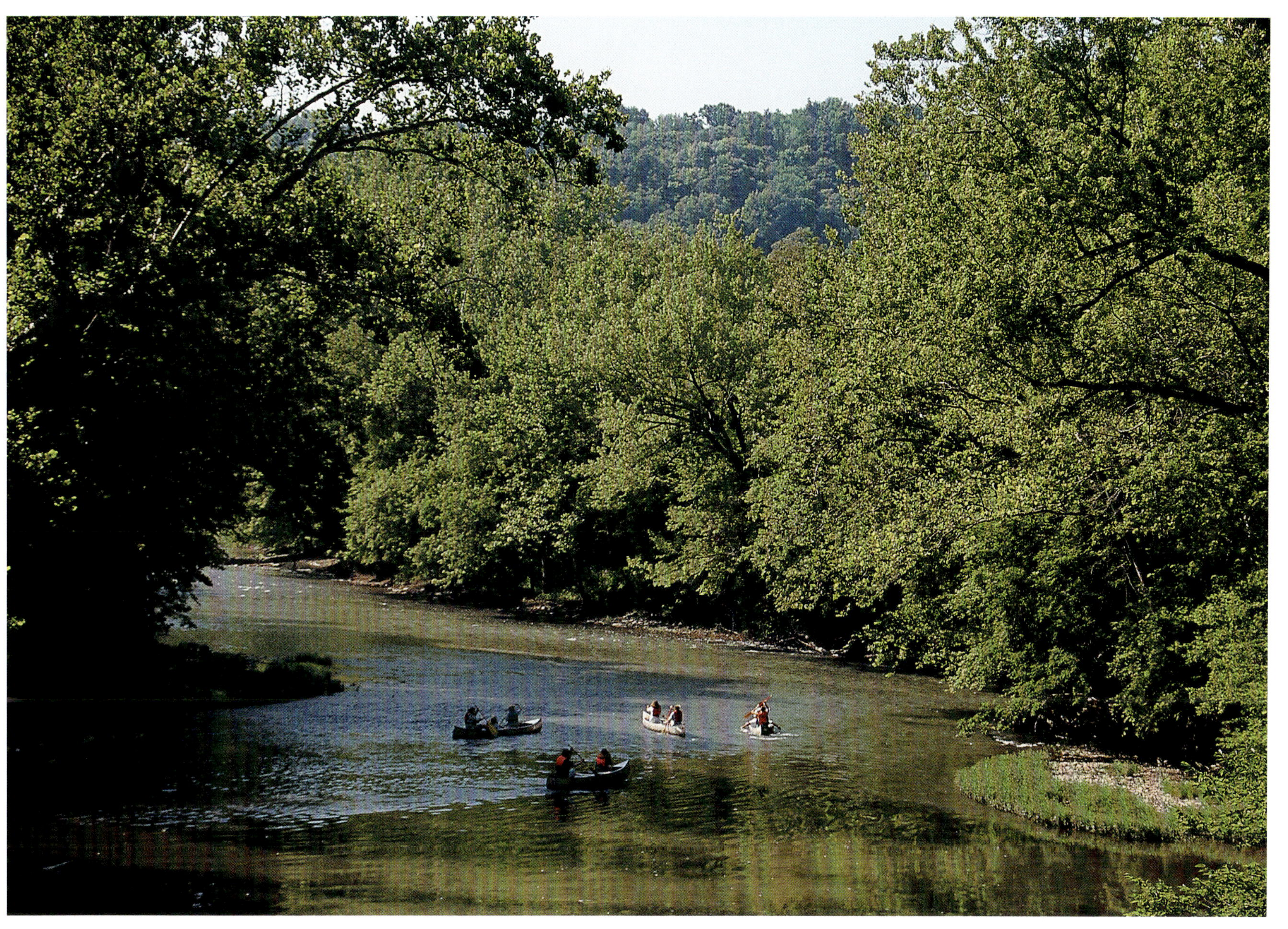

Flowing more than 100 miles from Clark County to the Ohio River, the Little Miami River offers 86 miles of pristine canoe routes. The river itself and the historic sites along its banks are protected by several state parks and a national scenic river designation.

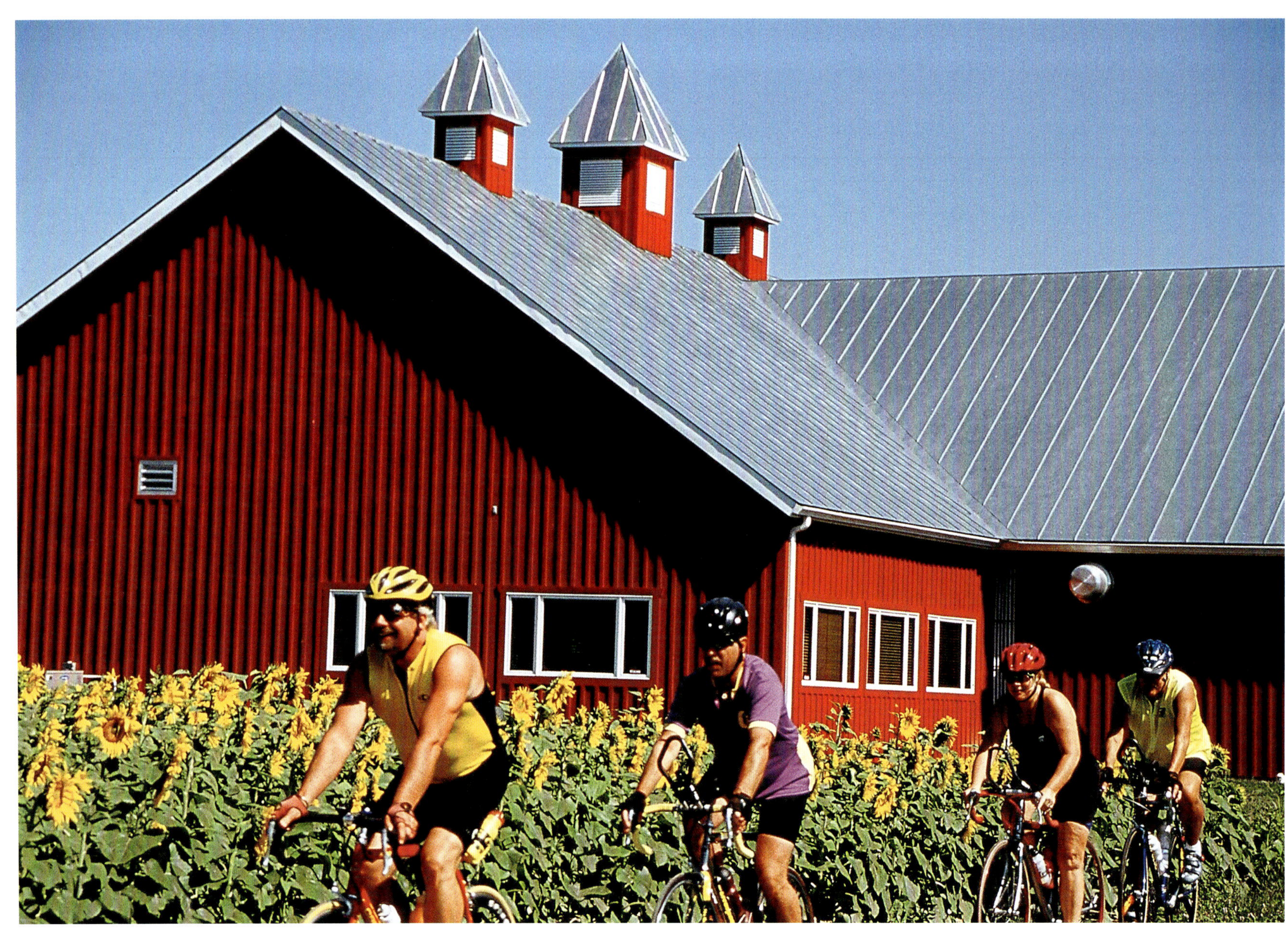

Cyclists and hikers can follow an abandoned railway line, now a paved route, for 69 miles along the Little Miami River. The route winds past rolling farmland, historic mills, and ancient native sites.

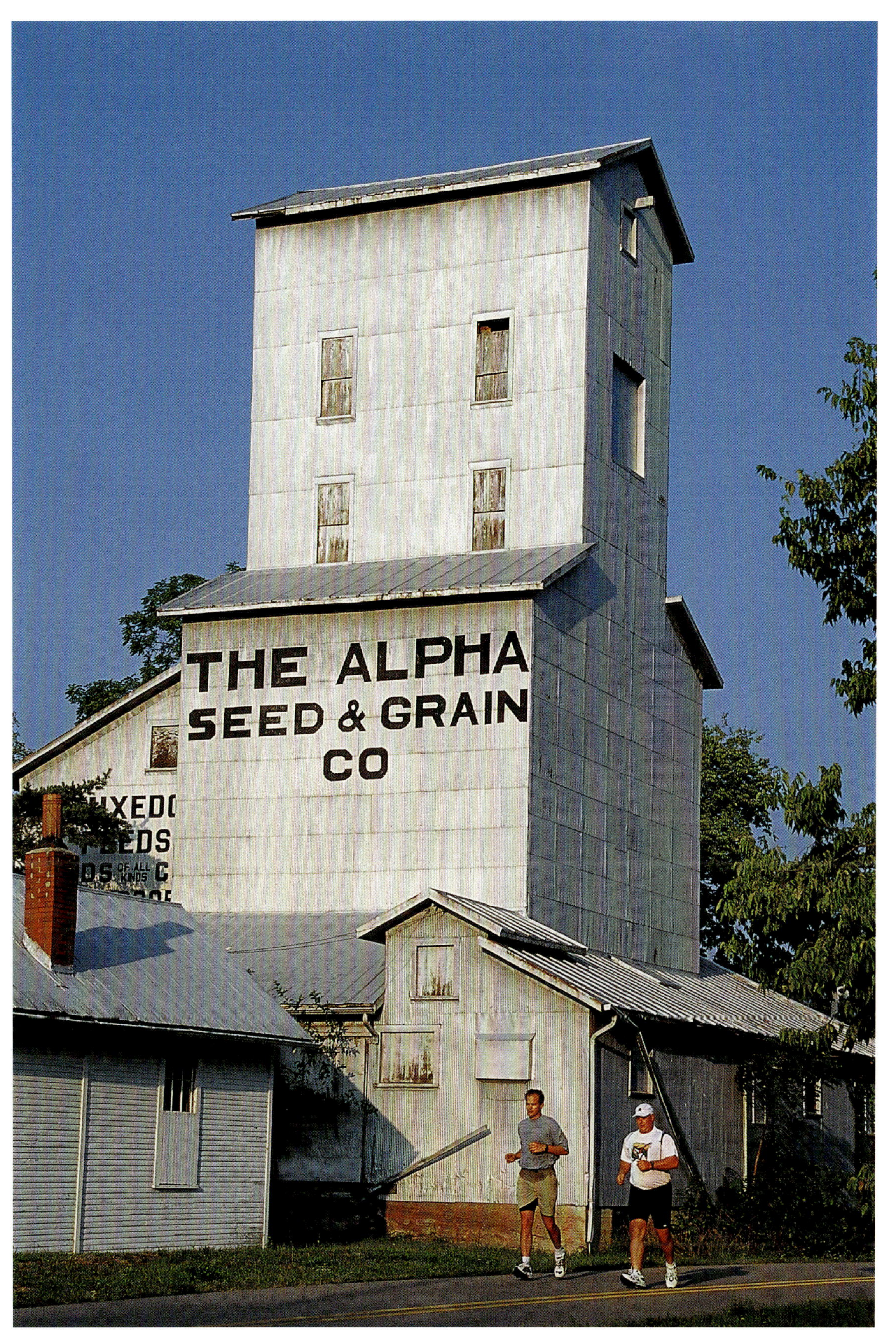

The Hopewell people were the first known inhabitants of the Little Miami River valley, gathering here between AD 300 and 600. The river is named for the Miami people, who, along with the Shawnee, lived here when the region was first settled by Europeans.

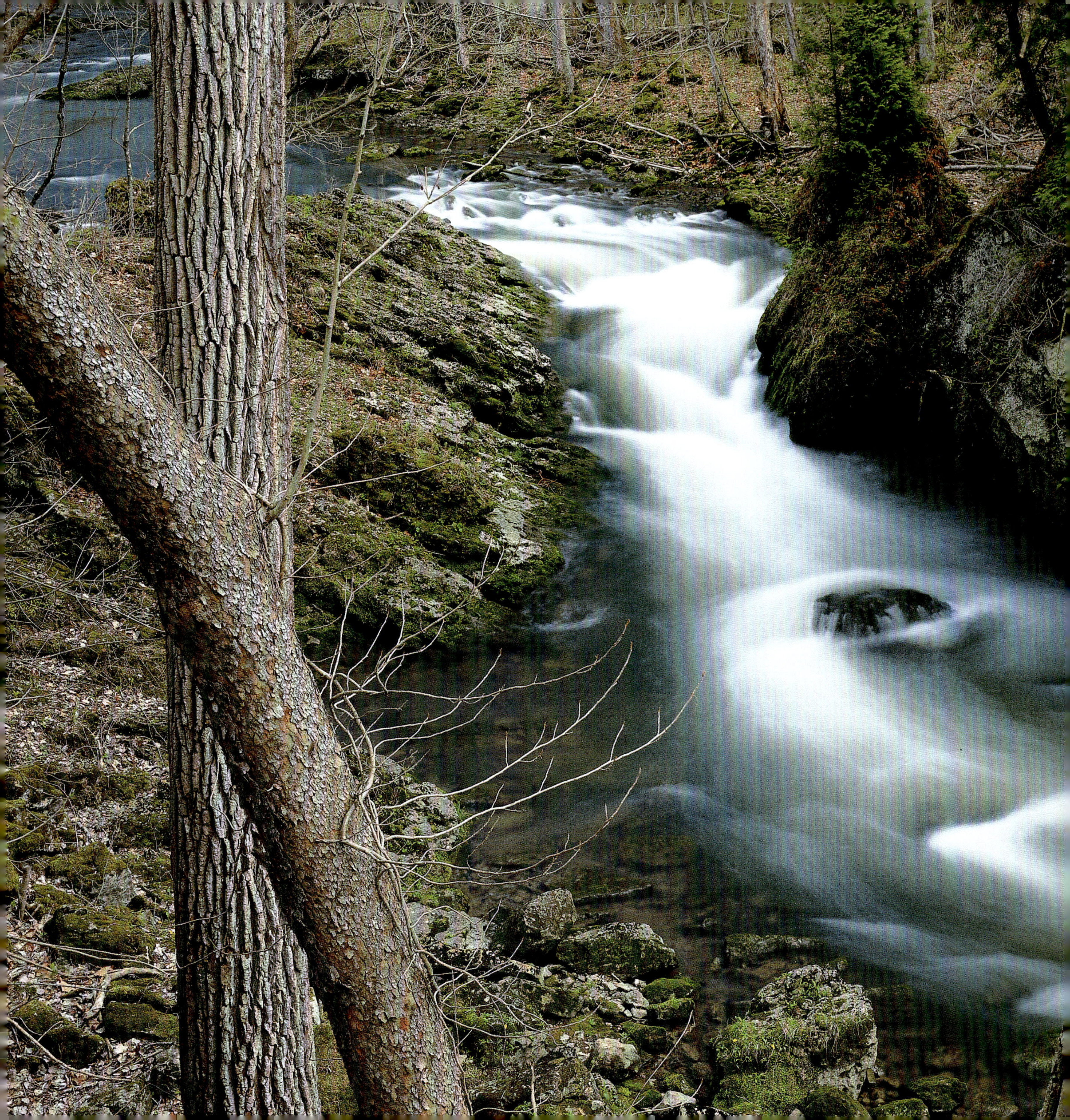

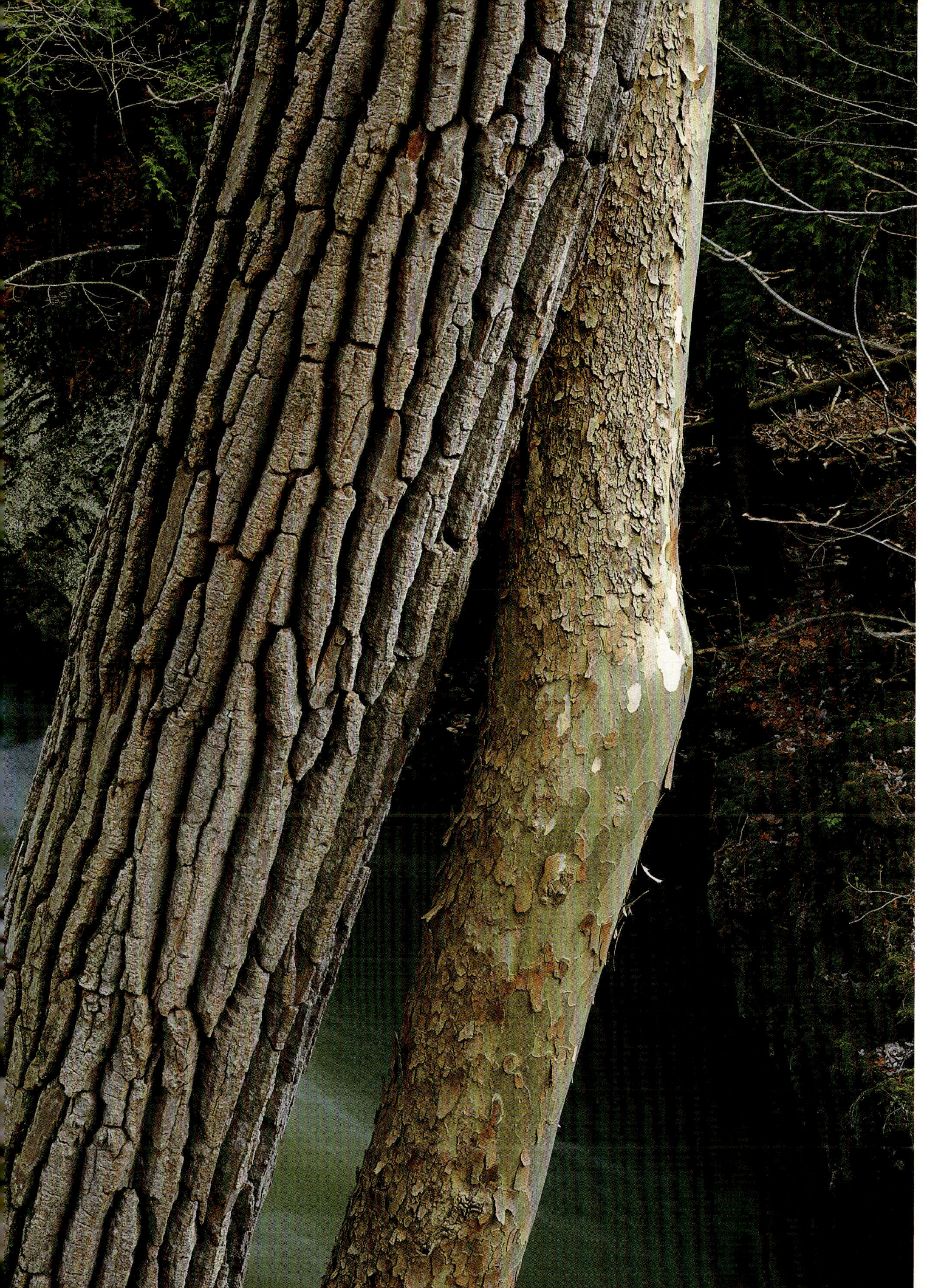

In Clifton Gorge State Nature Preserve the Little Miami River flows through deep ravines and potholes carved by the glaciers of past ice ages. The limestone and dolomite formations inspired the government to protect the region in 1968.

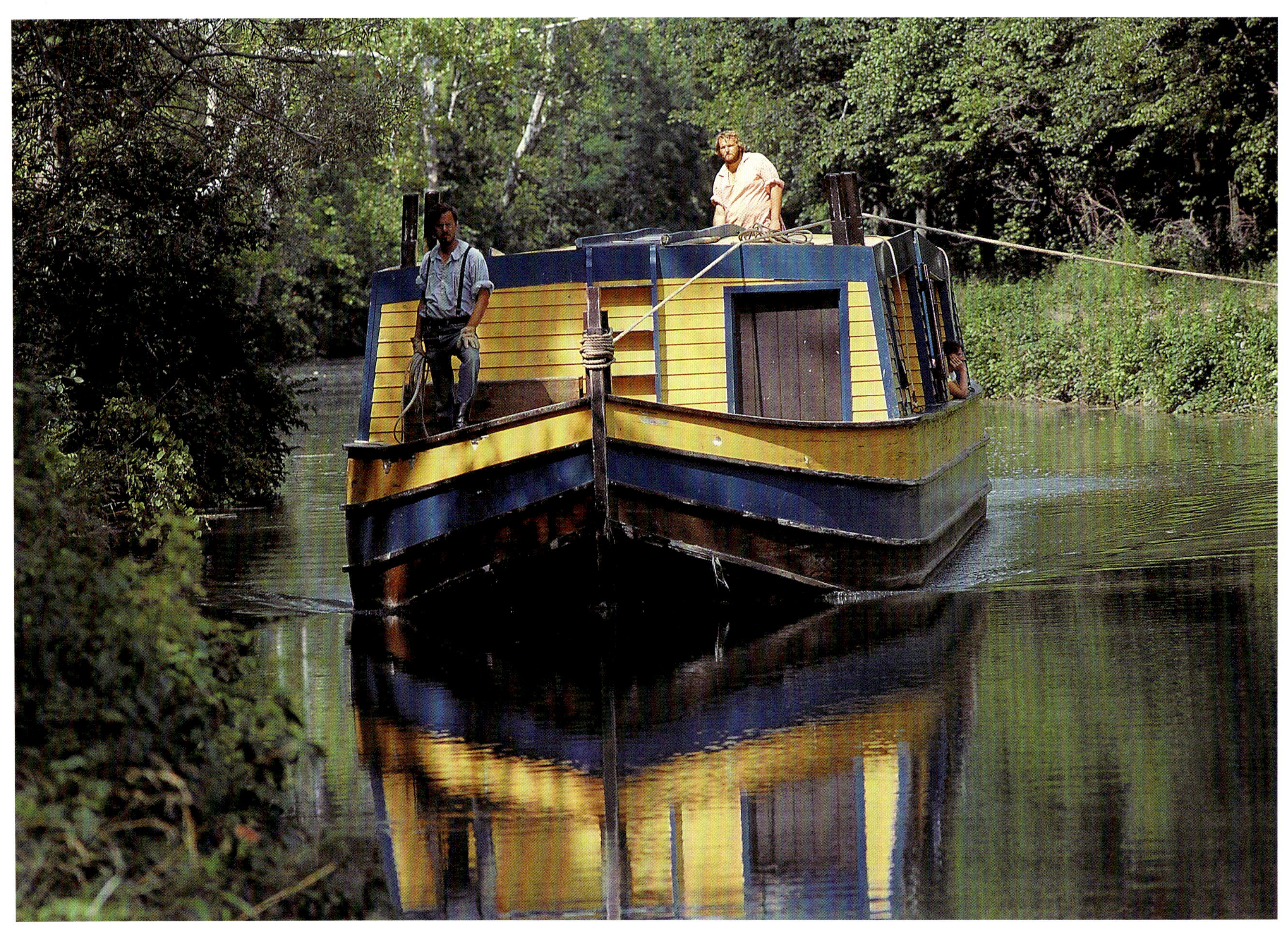

In the early 1800s, Ohio's government embarked on a major canal-building project for transporting the state's agricultural goods. One of these canals was the Miami & Erie, built between 1828 and 1845. Major floods in 1913 destroyed much of the network, and many of the remaining canals are now historic sites.

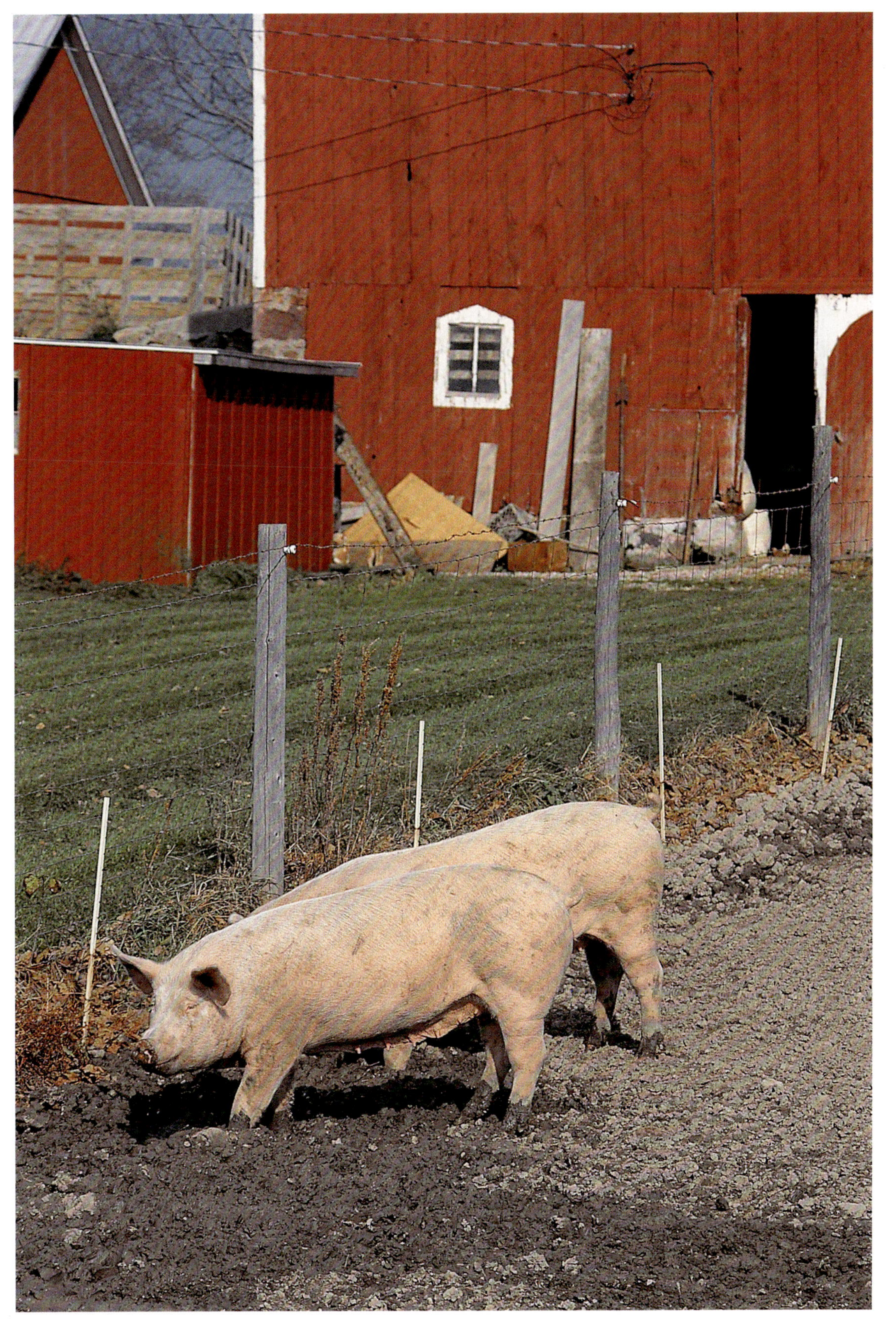

Pigs are big business here — Ohio is ninth in the nation for pig and hog production. A typical year might find 1.4 million hogs in pens around the state.

Two of Dayton's most famous residents — who gave the city its nickname the Birthplace of Aviation — were Orville and Wilbur Wright, bicycle builders determined to discover the secrets of flight. They succeeded in 1903 when their flying machine took to the air in Kitty Hawk, North Carolina.

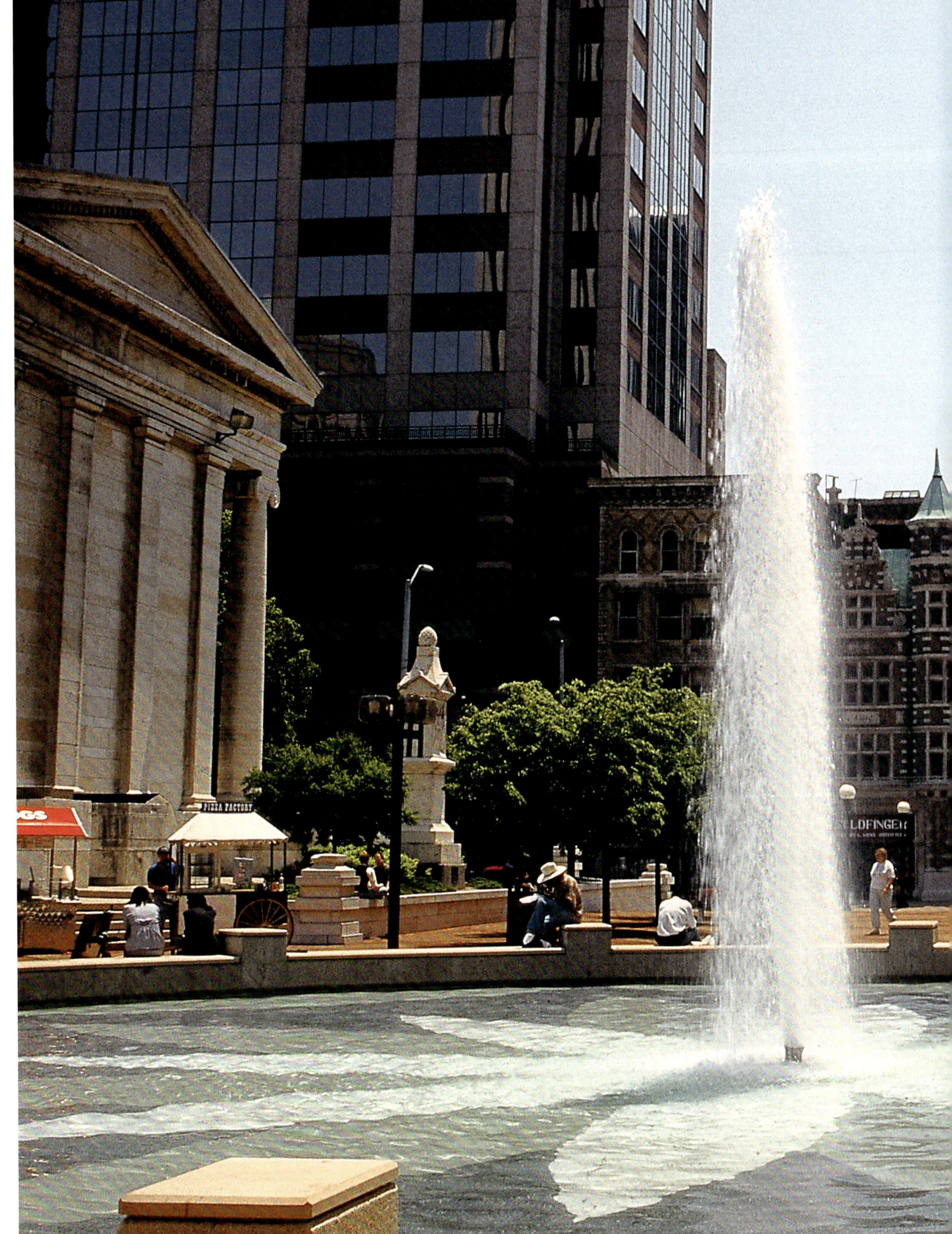

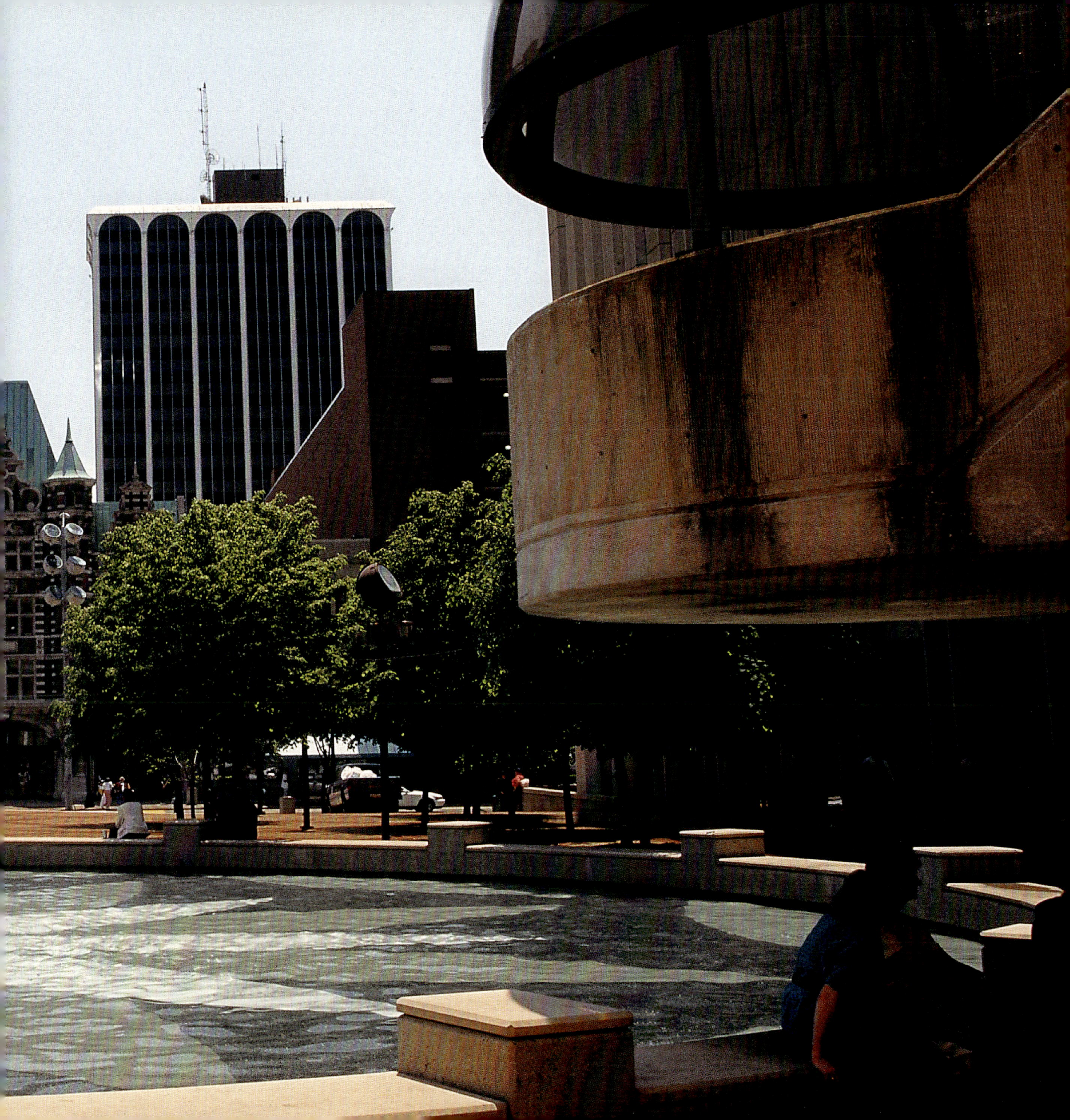

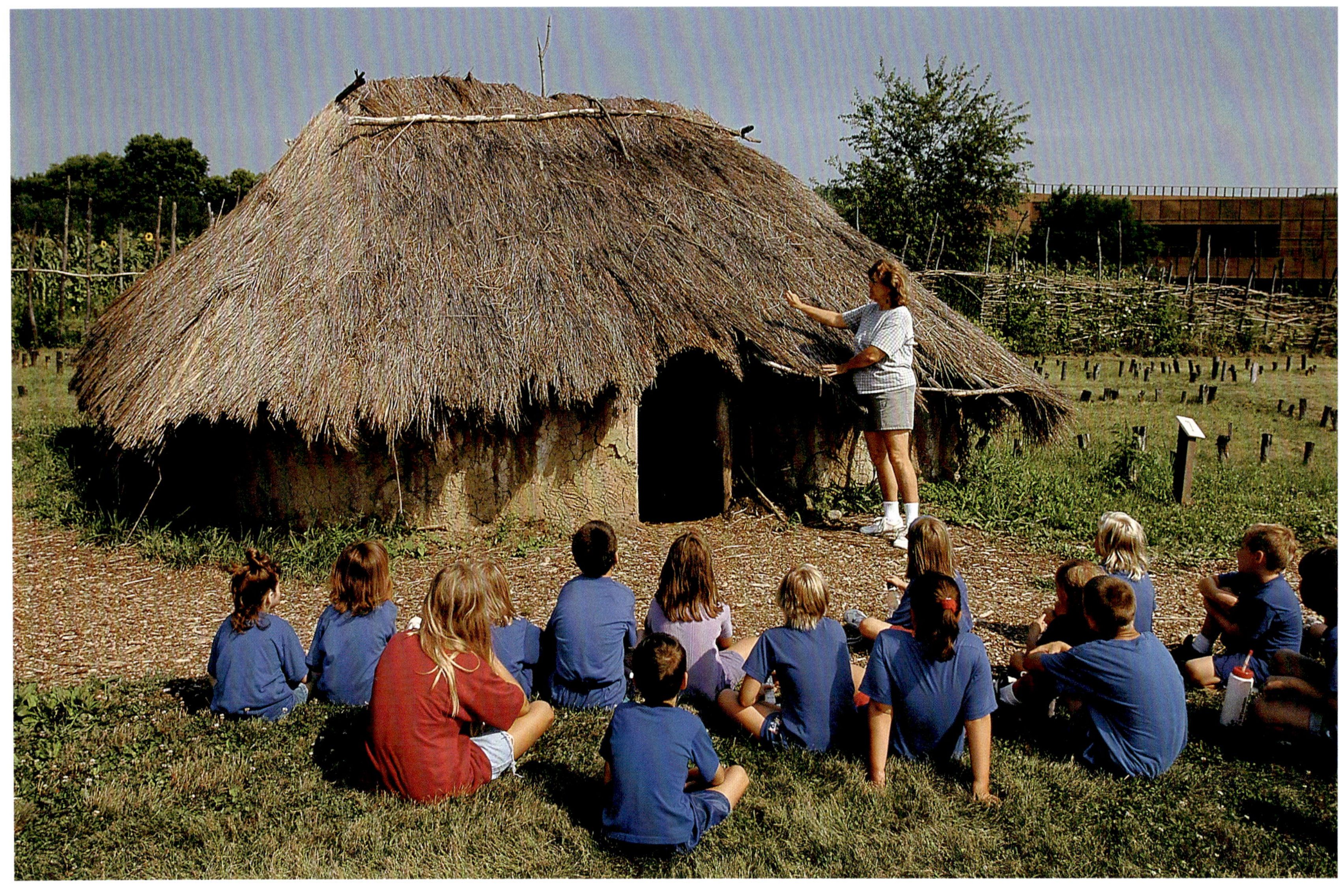

Children at the SunWatch Indian Village near Dayton spend a day discovering the customs of the Fort Ancient people who lived on the shores of the Great Miami River almost a century ago. The settlement is named for an elaborate wooden structure that acts as a sundial.

At the world's oldest, largest military aviation museum, sightseers discover the history of flight through more than 300 planes and missiles. About 1.5 million visitors tour the United States Air Force Museum in Dayton each year.

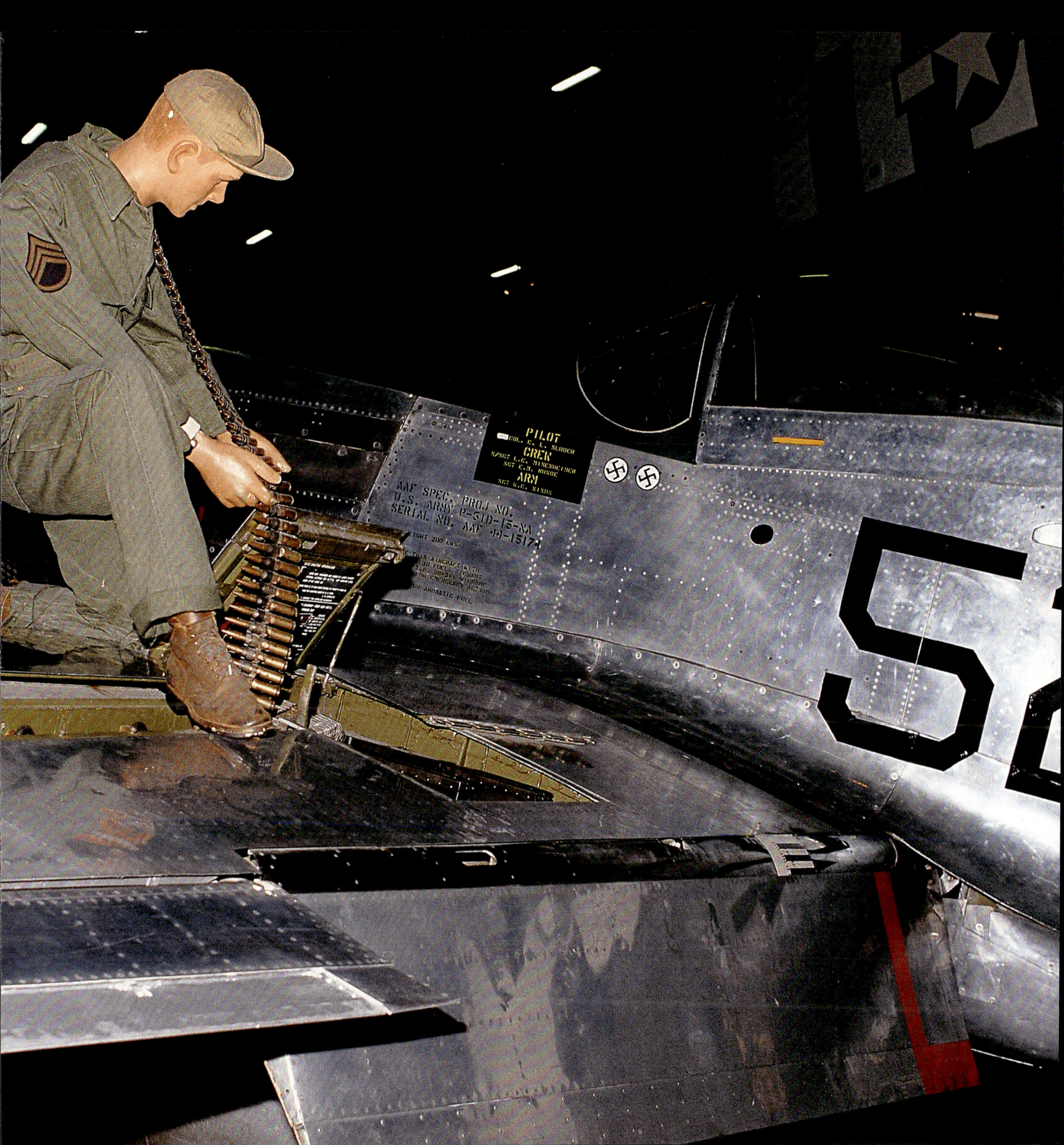
PILOT
COL. C. L. SLUDER
CREW
ARM
AAF SPEC. PROJ NO.
U.S. ARMY P-51D-15-NA
SERIAL NO. AAF 44-15174
5

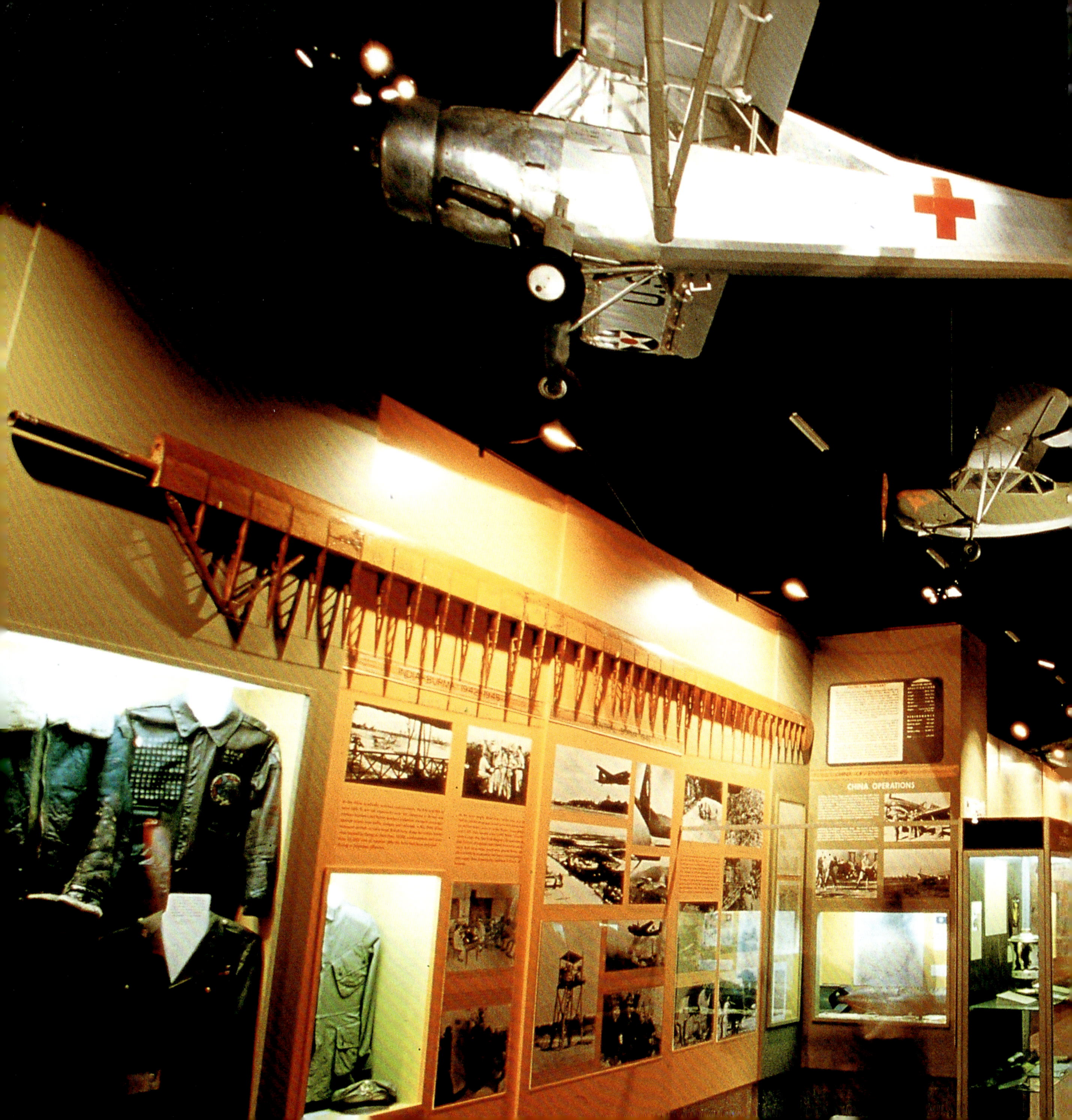
INDIA-BURMA 1942-1945
CHINA OPERATIONS

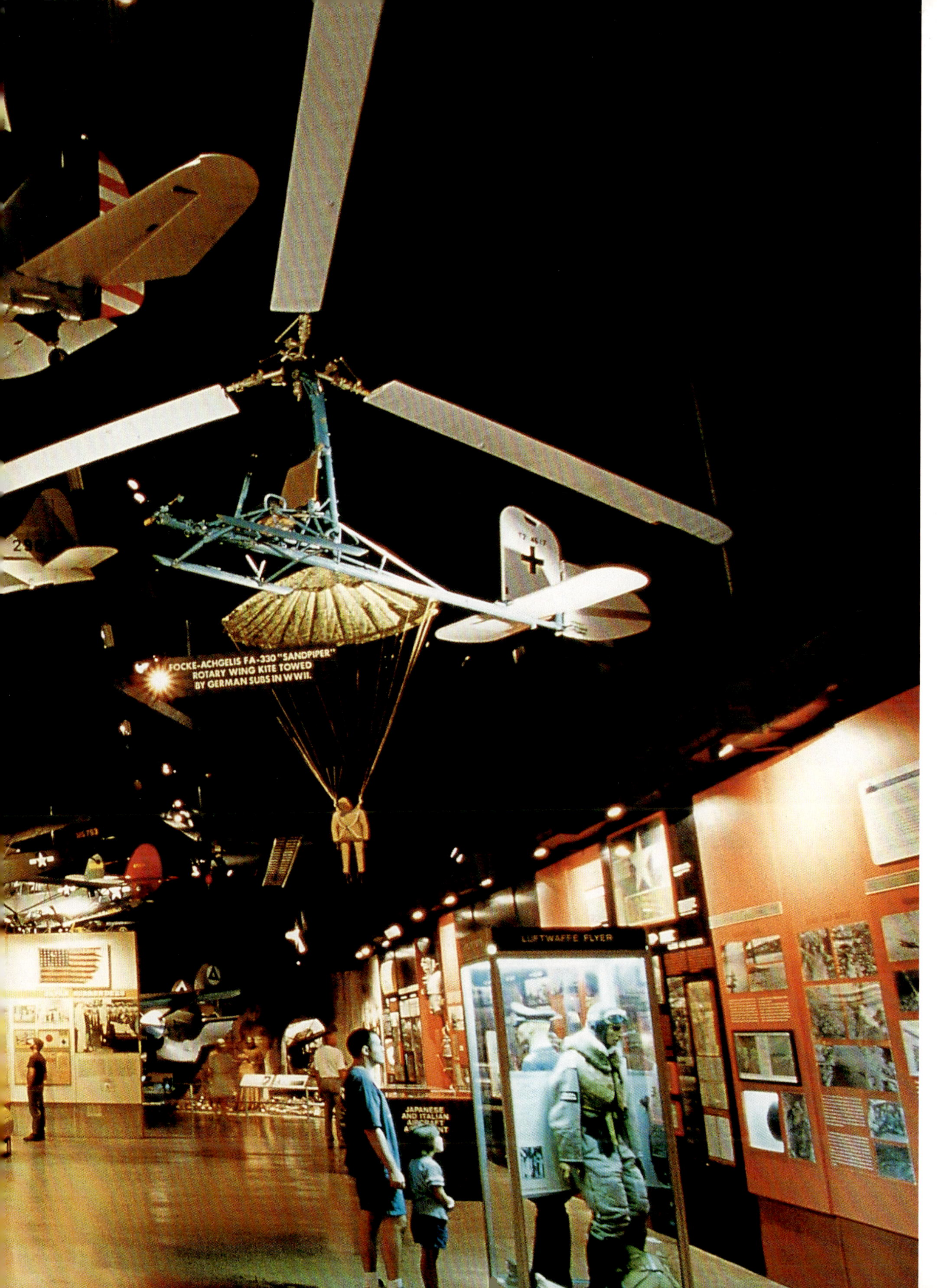

The largest air force base in the United States, Wright-Patterson is one of the world's leading aeronautical research centers. About 24,000 people work here, in management, flight operations, education, and other areas.

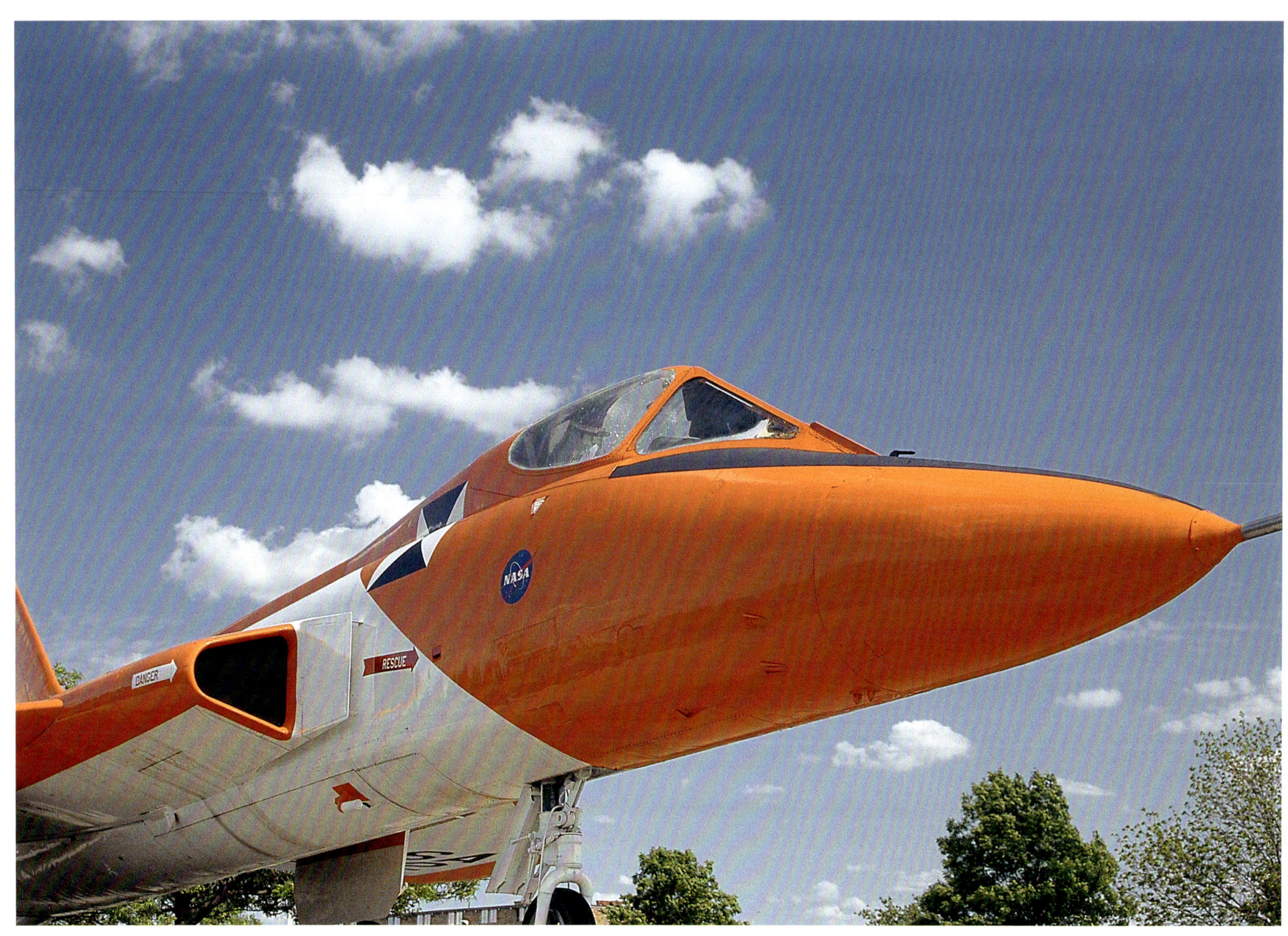

Neil Armstrong, the first man to walk on the moon, was born on August 5, 1930, near Wapakoneta, Ohio. The city is now home to the Neil Armstrong Air and Space Museum, created in 1972 in the astronaut's honor.

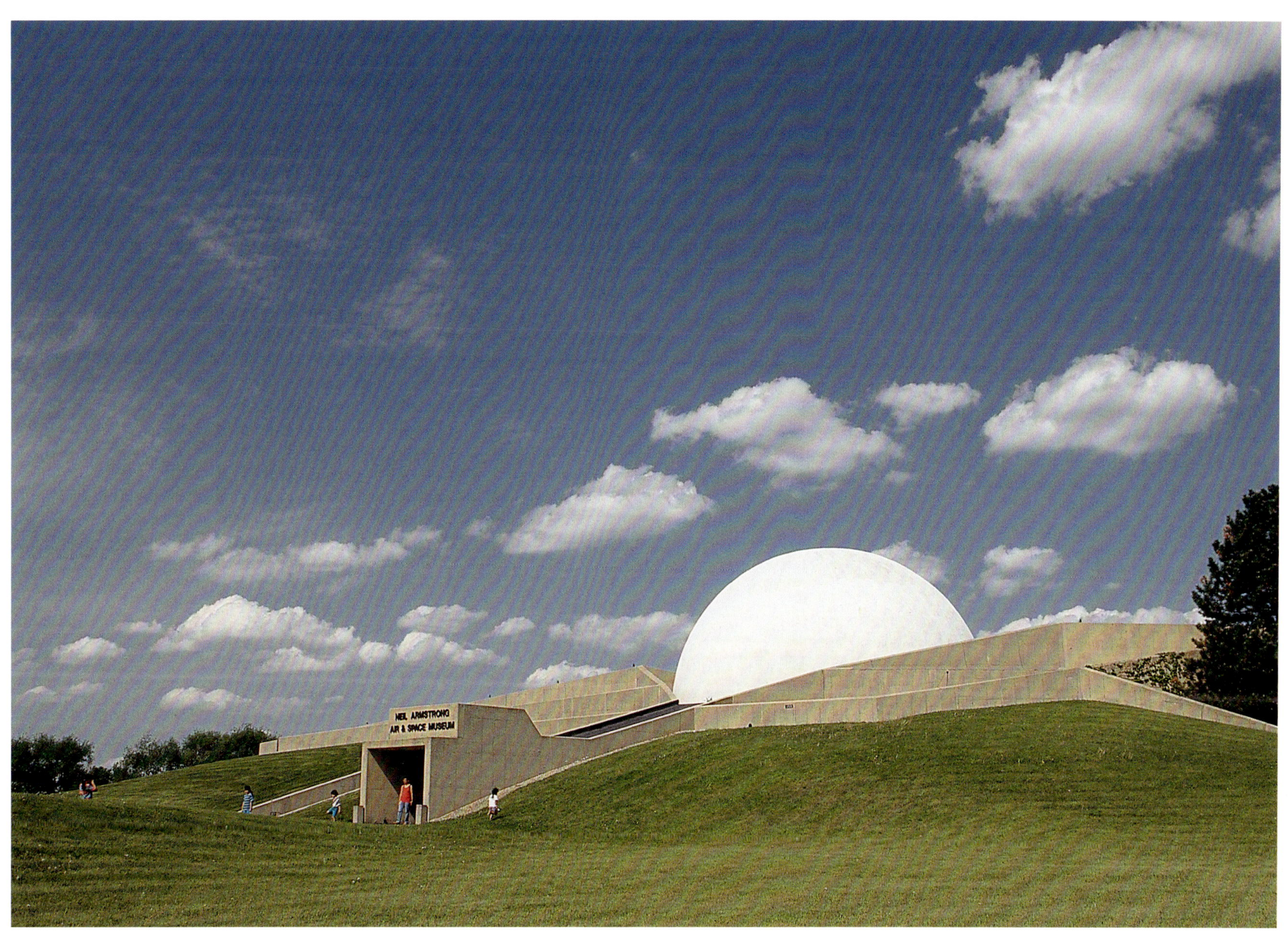

Visitors to the Neil Armstrong Air and Space Museum can view the Gemini 8 Spacecraft, a landing simulator, space suits once worn by Neil Armstrong, a moon rock, and much more.

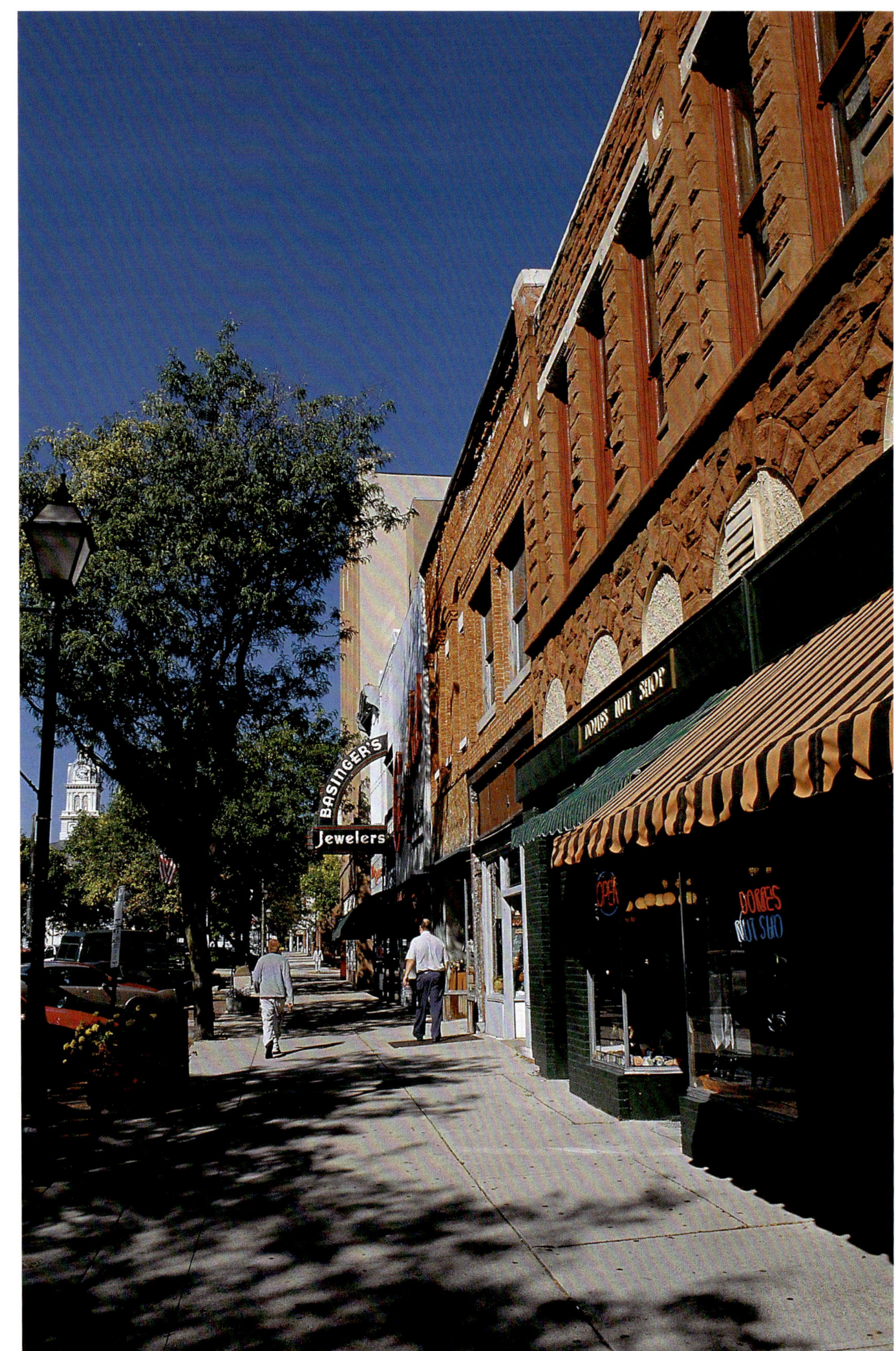

Settled in the early 1800s, Lima was named for Lima, Peru, a source of quinine. Ohio's early residents needed the substance to treat what they called "swamp fever," now better known as malaria.

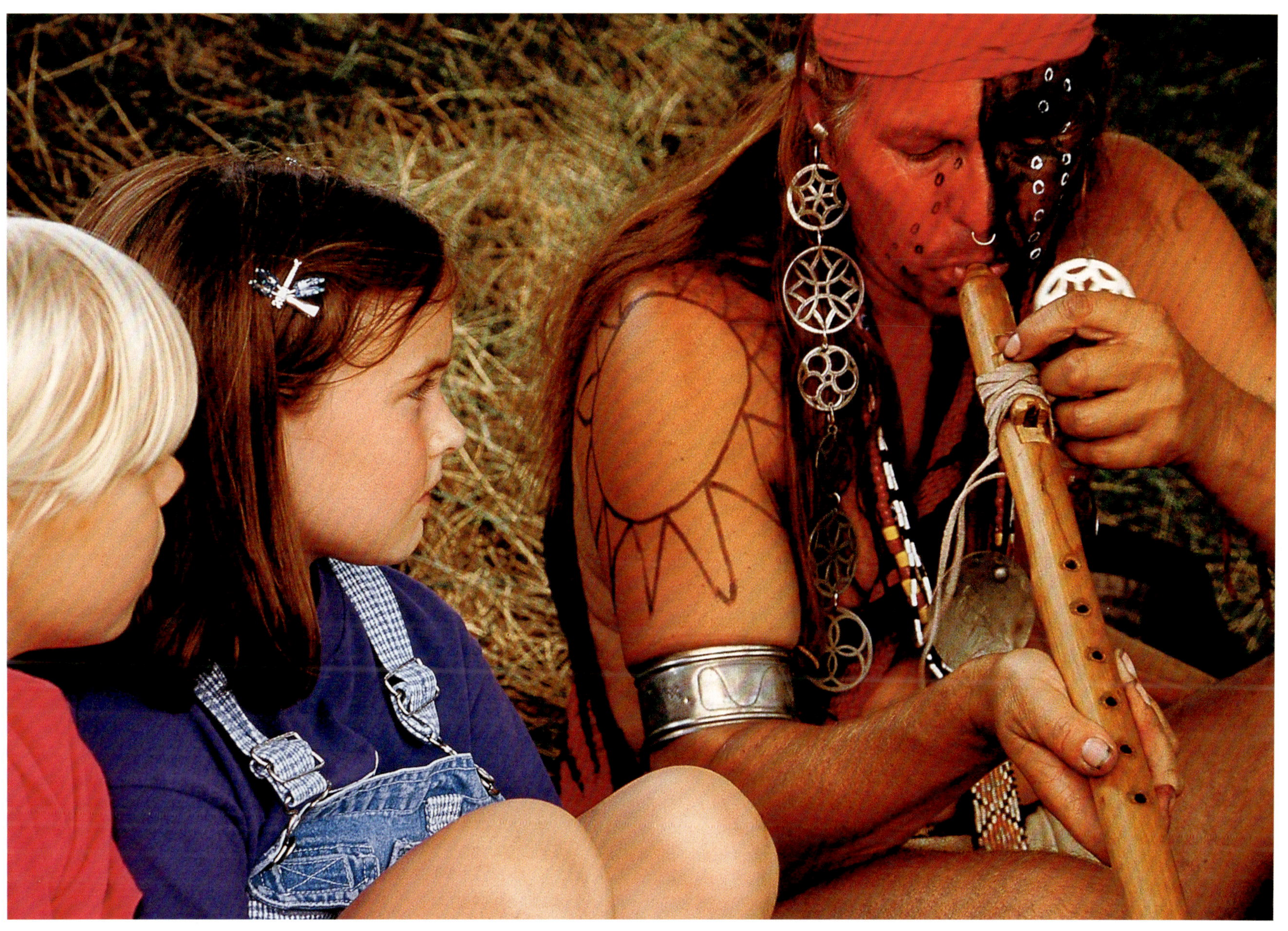

Between May and October, visitors to Fort Meigs may find themselves in the midst of musket fire as actors re-enact battles of Ohio's early days. The fort was built in 1813 and today's replica is the largest wooden fortification on the continent.

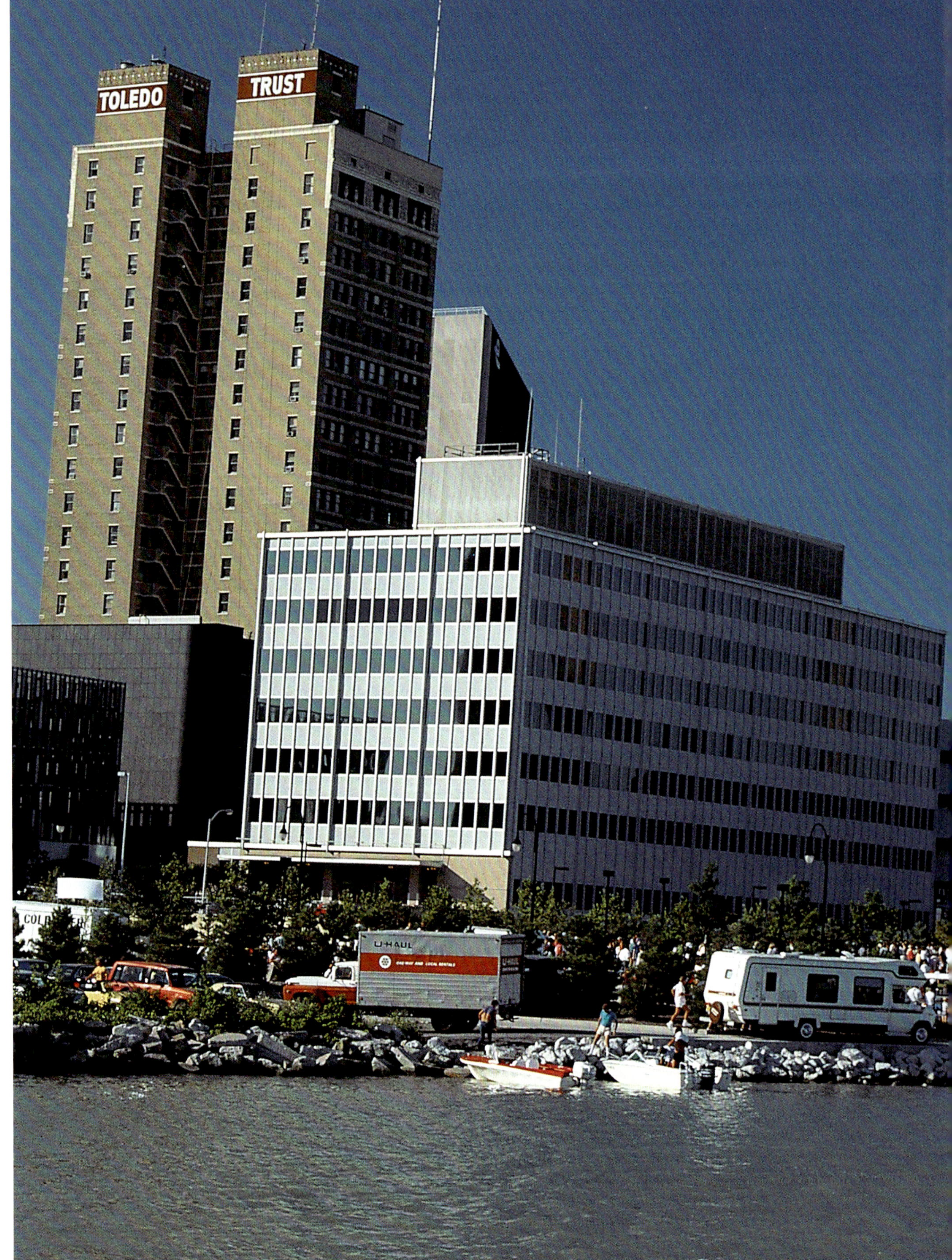

Toledo's access to the St. Lawrence Seaway has made it a major shipping port and a natural center for industry. Glass, automobiles, plastic, and machinery are manufactured here.

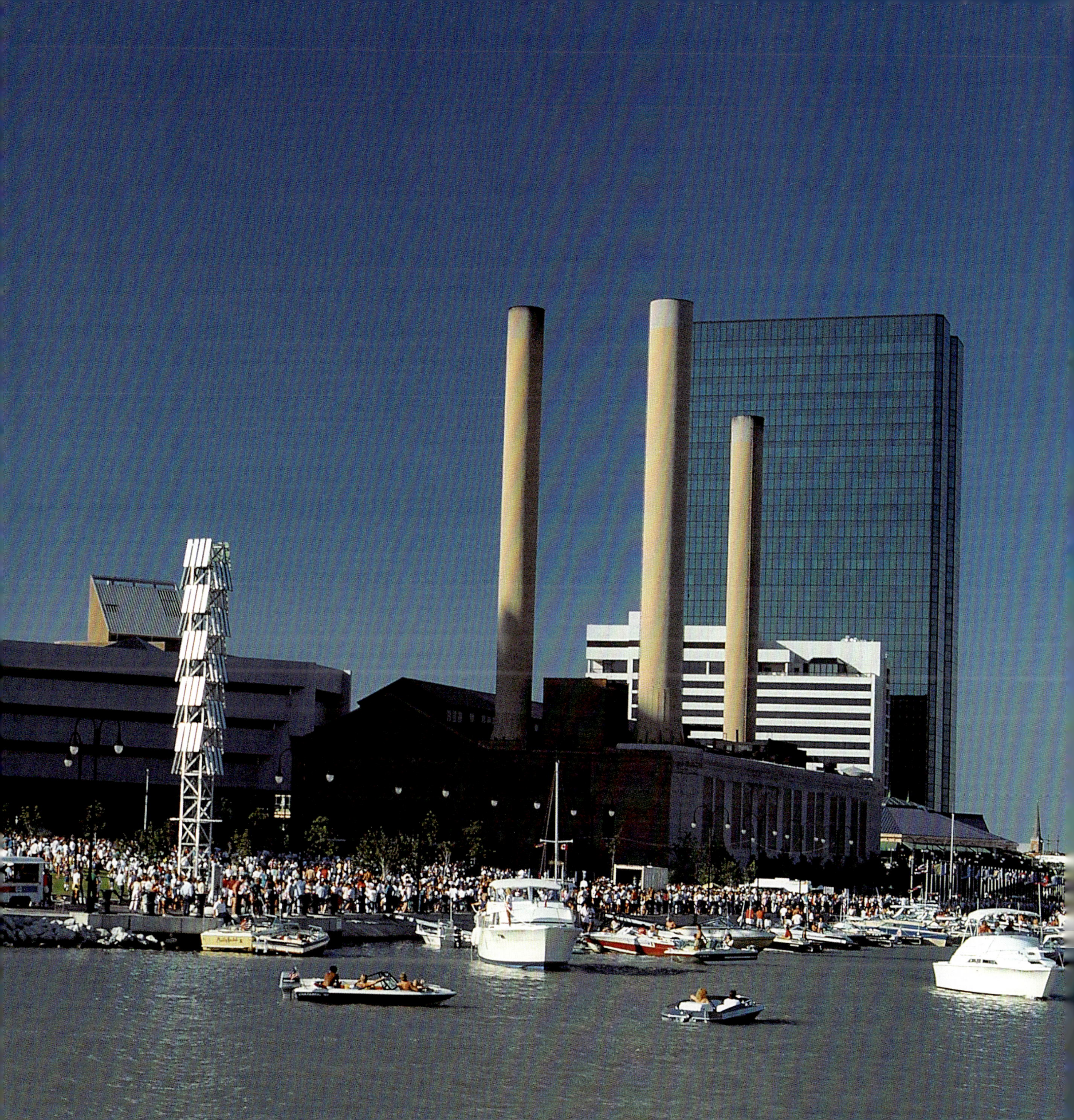

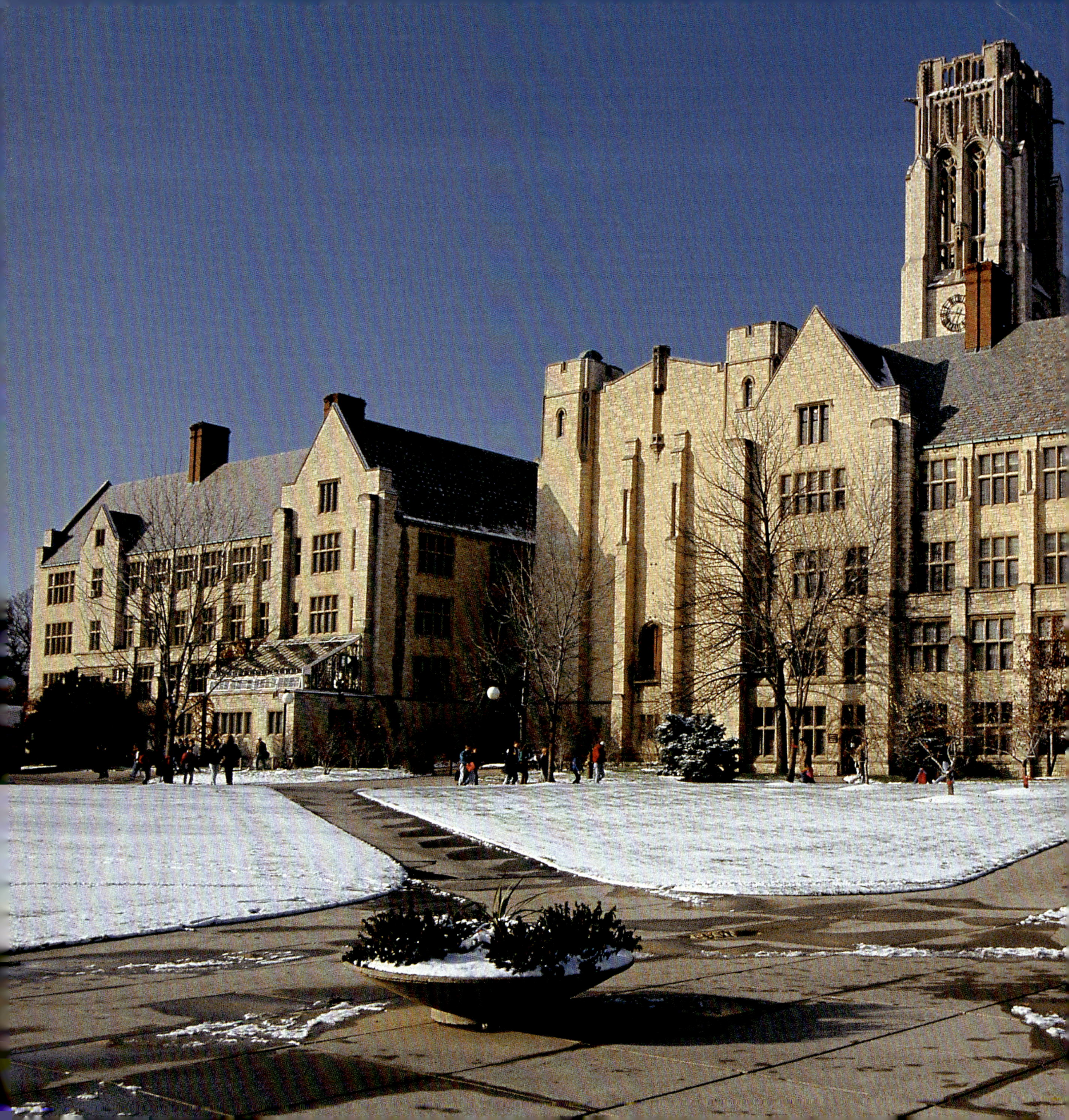

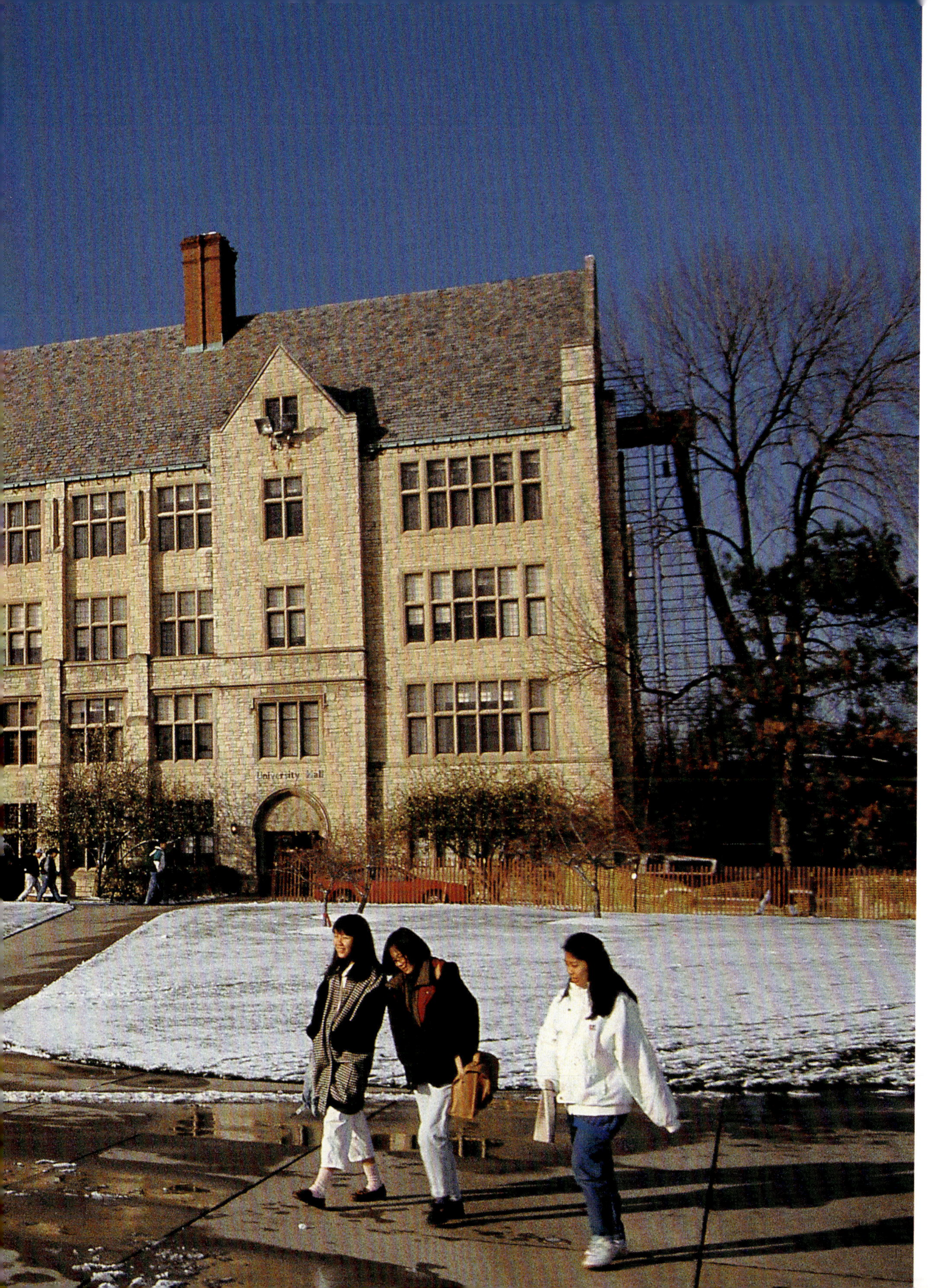

Toledo resident Jesup W. Scott believed the city should provide its youth with education, and he put his beliefs into practice in 1872 with a 160-acre endowment, now the University of Toledo. About 20,500 students attend classes here.

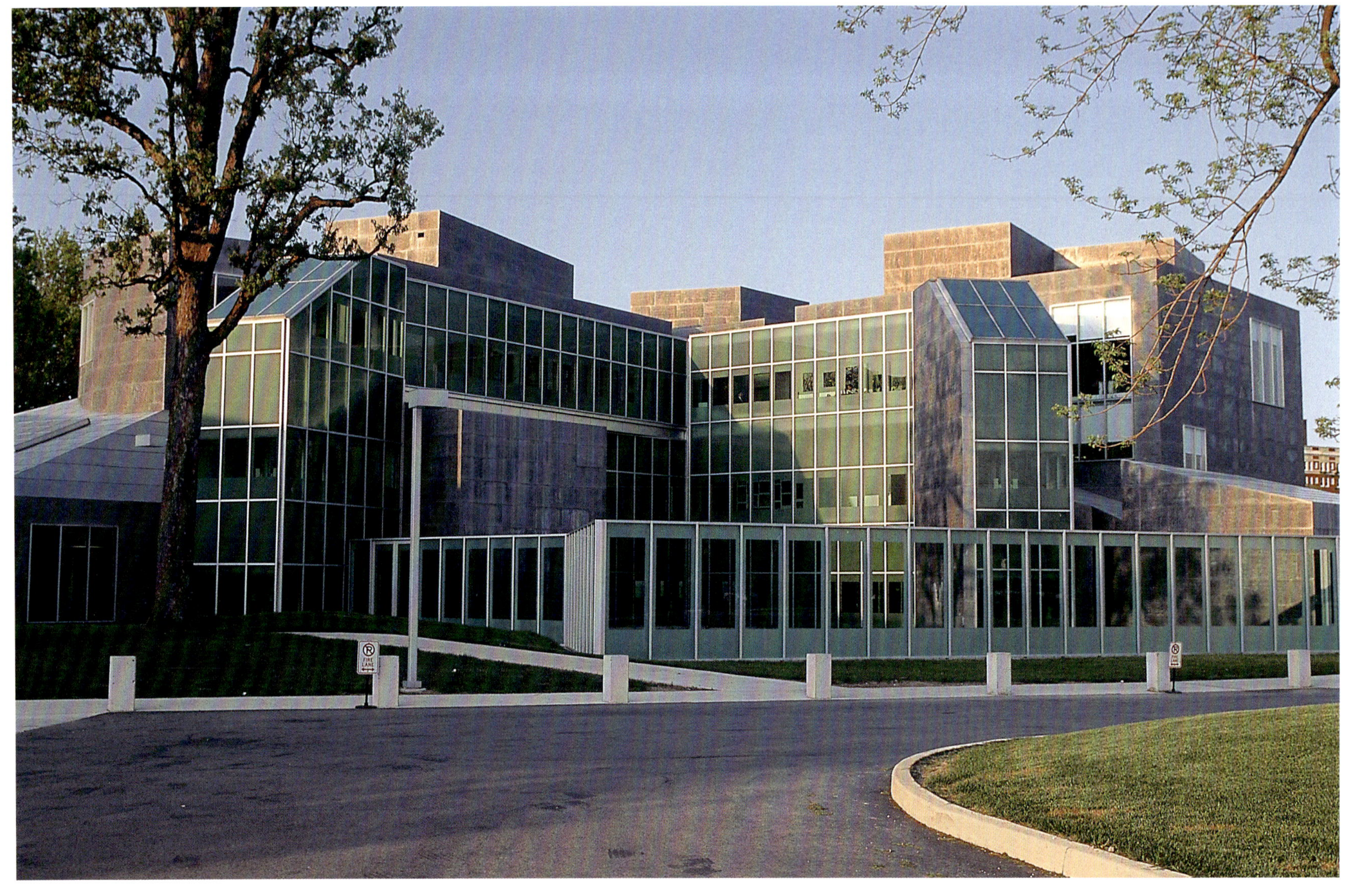

Founded in 1901 by Edward Drummond Libbey, owner of the Libbey Glass Company, the Toledo Museum of Art takes pride in having one of the largest glass collections in the world. Visitors can see examples of American, European, and ancient glass-making techniques.

Ohio farmers harvest more than a million acres of wheat each year, along with plentiful crops of soybeans, corn, and hay.

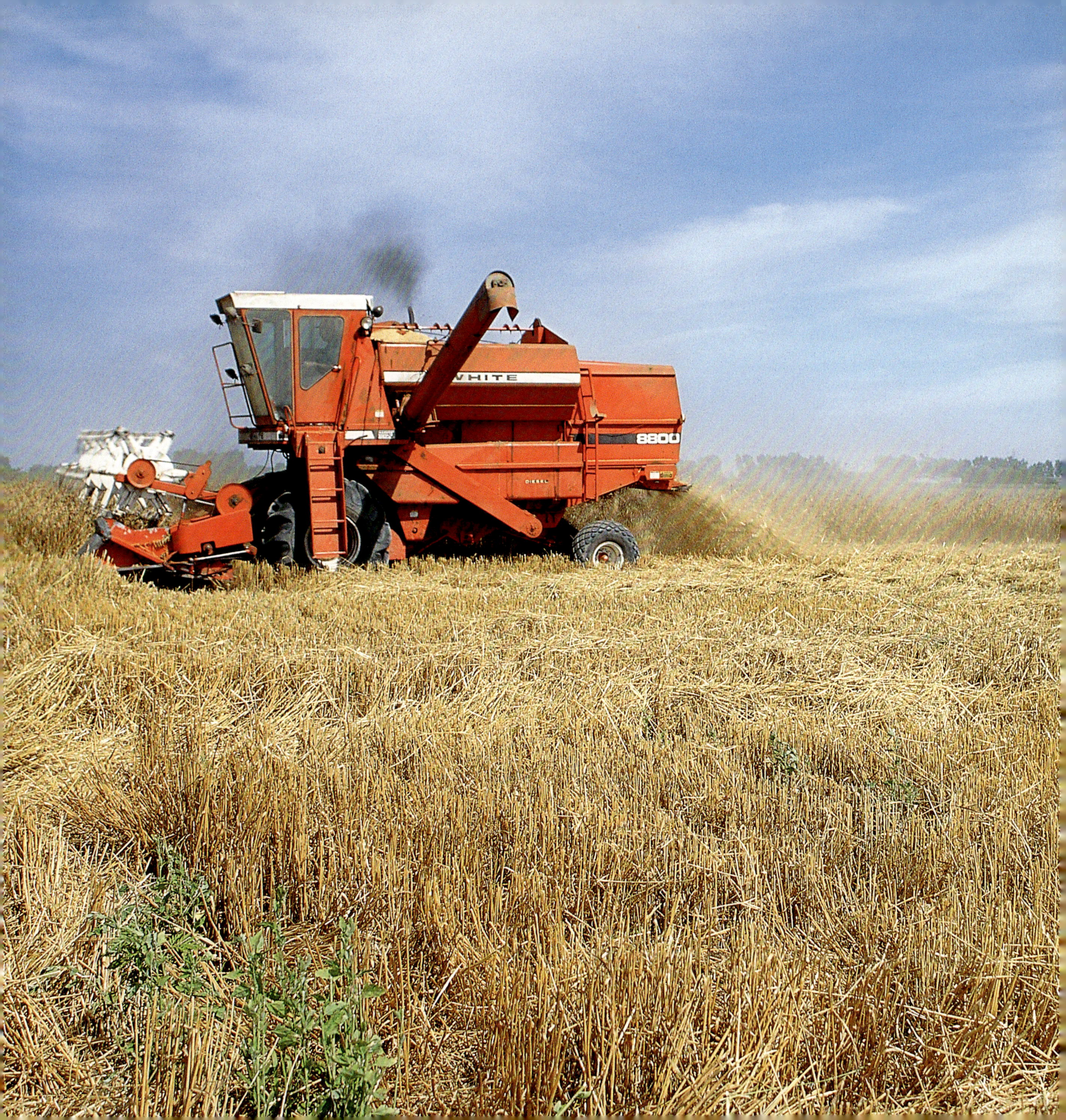
8800
DIESEL

One in six Ohio residents are employed by the agriculture industry, either farming itself or related jobs such as marketing, processing, or retailing. In total, the industry adds $67.7 billion annually to the economy.

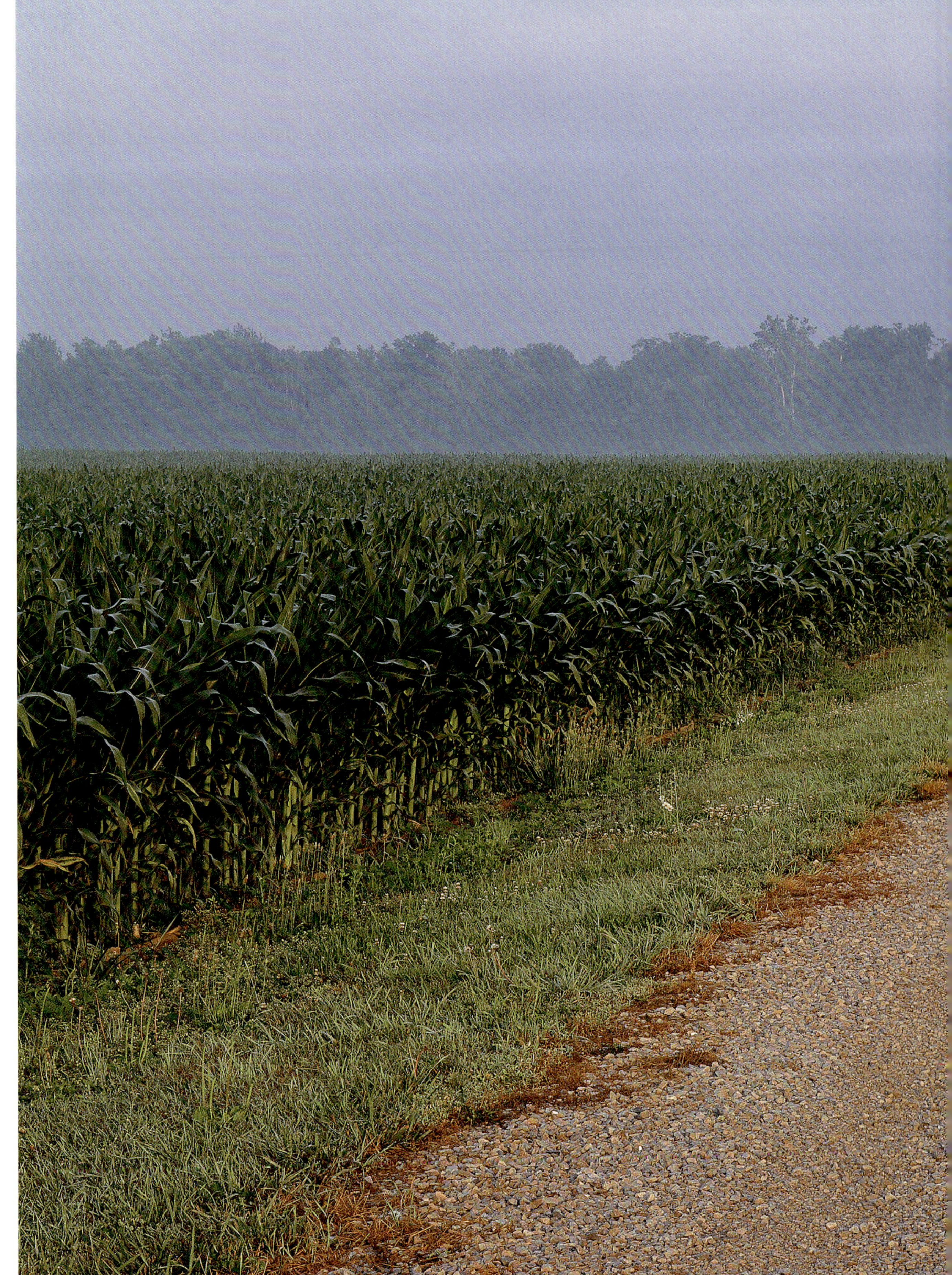

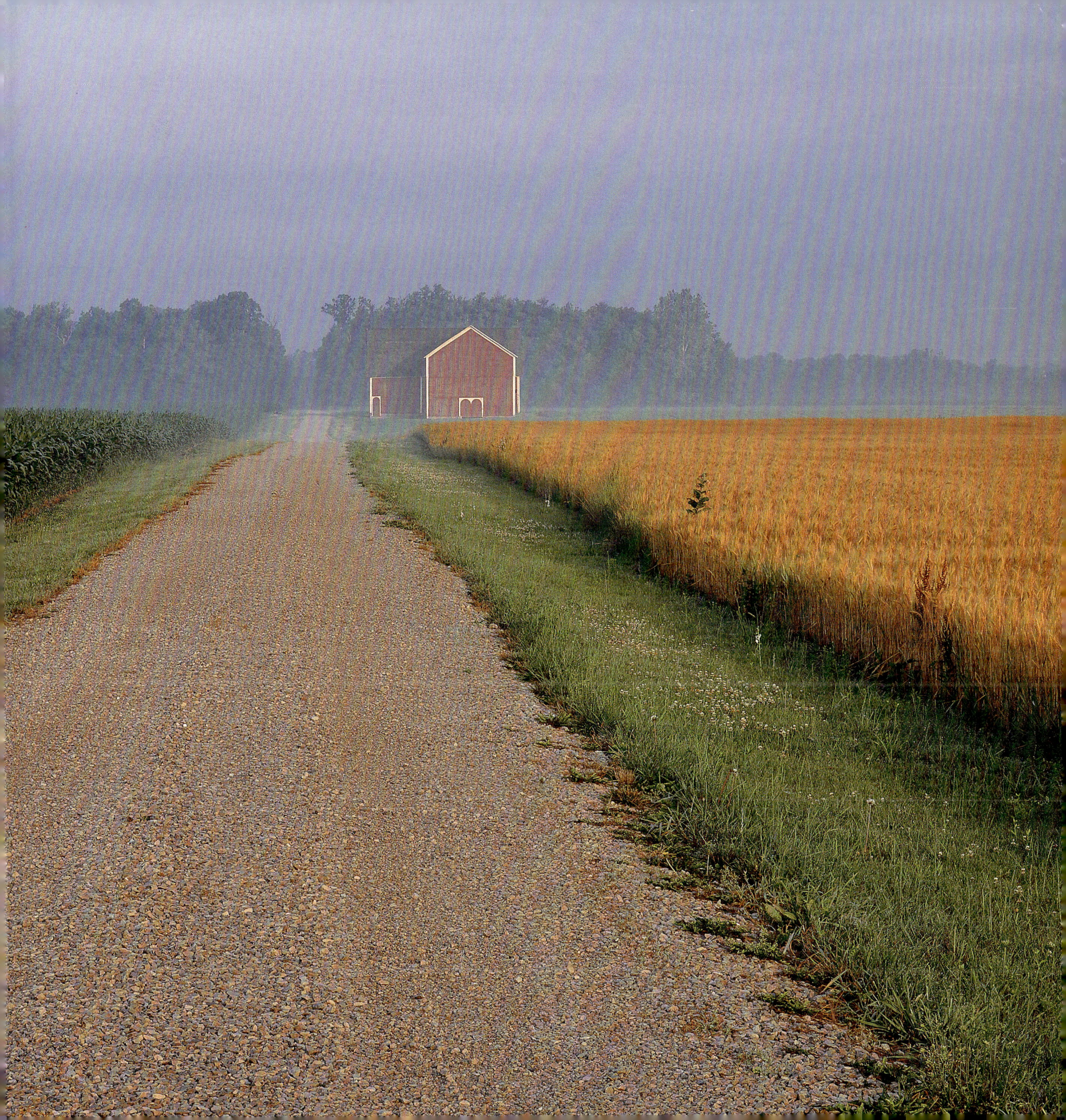

Photo Credits

G. Alan Nelson/Dembinsky Photo Assoc 1, 3, 16, 18–19, 30–31, 54–55, 94–95

Tom Till 6–7, 21, 47, 48–49, 51, 52, 57, 60–61, 67

Jeff Greenberg/Unicorn Stock Photos 8, 10, 42, 44–45, 50, 80

Jeff Greenberg/Folio, Inc. 9, 26–27, 28, 37, 46, 72, 73

Al Messerschmidt/Folio, Inc. 11

B. W. Hoffmann/Unicorn Stock Photos 12–13, 15

Mark E. Gibson/Dembinsky Photo Assoc 14, 63, 65

Jeff Greenberg/Photri Inc. 17, 71, 82–83, 87

Jim Roetzel/Dembinsky Photo Assoc 20

Jean Higgins/Unicorn Stock Photos 22, 23, 43

Robert W. Ginn/Unicorn Stock Photos 24

Jürgen Vogt 25, 33, 40–41, 56, 58, 59, 64, 66, 86

Daniel J. Olson/Unicorn Stock Photos 29, 39

Dennis Johnson/Folio, Inc. 32, 36

Mark Romesser/Unicorn Stock Photos 34–35

Andre Jenny/Unicorn Stock Photos 38, 78–79, 84, 85, 92

Darryl R. Beers/Dembinsky Photo Assoc 53

Ed Lallo/Mach 2 Stock Exchange 62

David R. Frazier/Folio, Inc. 68–69

Ron Goulet/Dembinsky Photo Assoc 70

Willard Clay/Dembinsky Photo Assoc 74–75

James P. Rowan 76

Larime Photo/Dembinsky Photo Assoc 77

Russell R. Grundke/Unicorn Stock Photos 81

Eugene L. Drifmeyer/Photri Inc. 88–89

Chromosohm/Unicorn Stock Photos 90–91

Randall B. Henne/Dembinsky Photo Assoc 93